HOW TO BECOME A SUCCESSFUL EVENT PLANNER

A Practical Approach to Starting and Running Your Own Event Planning Business from Home

JORGE ZURITA

HOW TO BECOME A SUCCESSFUL EVENT PLANNER

ISBN: 0615456588
ISBN-13: 9780615456584

*To my wife Monica, my son Jorge and
my daughter Sandra: the greatest events that
ever happened to me. With you, every day is a party.*

With all my love,

Jorge

SURPRISE!

(FREE GIFTS – Just for you)

As my way of thanking you for purchasing this book, I'm going to give you a very special pack of digital bonuses that will help you bigtime on your journey to becoming a successful event planner.

Here's what you're about to download:

- **The quick-start guide to starting your event planning business**
  Discover how to get started quickly and easily and what steps to take on your way to success without losing direction or wasting valuable resources.

- **Expert event selling secrets**
  How to always be your prospect's first choice by doing what you know and knowing what you do like nobody else.

- **The event-planning pitfall report**
  You'll learn the 23 most common mistakes, blunders and pitfalls that new event planners make... this one is a true deal-saver.

- **The supply negotiator YES manual**
  I'll share with you over twenty different techniques to close the best deals with your product and service suppliers.

- **The secret event planning black book**
  A small collection of online tools that will help your day-to-day operations and boost your event planning business to the big leagues.

- **The event planner glossary**
  This handy-dandy report will help you to know and master the terminology and secret slang of the event planning industry.

- And much more...

- To **grab all these free gifts** and stay up to date on the latest tips, tricks, tactics and techniques of the event planning industry, all you need to do is join my insiders list by going online to www.MasteringEventPlanning.com

Praise for Jorge Zurita and
How to Become a Successful Event Planner

"*How to Become a Successful Event Planner* is full of wisdom and know-how. Both entrepreneurs who are just getting into the field as well as seasoned veterans will appreciate the comprehensive details that Jorge Zurita provides in his book."

Janet Elkins
President at Eventworks,Inc
www.eventworks.com

"Without a doubt, *How to Become a Successful Event Planner* is the most thorough and concise book that I have read on this topic. Although I am a 44 year veteran, I still picked up new tips from Jorge Zurita's book."

John J. Daly, Jr.
President at John Daly, Inc
www.jdalyinc.com

"I've been a professional event planner for more than 25-years, and this is one of the best books that I have ever read about the event planning industry.

Greg Jenkins
Partner at Bravo Productions
www.bravoevents-online.com

"Combined with actual work experience (a must!) *How to Become a Successful Event Planner* reveals how to start in the event business, and is an honest appraisal and road map to achieve success in this coveted profession".

Andrea Michaels
Author of the book: *Reflections of a Successful Wallflower: Lessons in Business; Lessons in Life*
CEO at Extraodinary Events
www.extraordinaryevents.net

"Jorge Zurita's *How To Become a Successful Event Planner*" provides lots of practical advice from someone who has worked in the trenches developing an independent meeting planning business. There are many good tips to be found here".

Corbin Ball, CSP, CMP
CEO at Corbin Ball Associates
www.corbinball.com

"Jorge has captured and articulated the special event planning business perfectly. His expertise and wealth of knowledge is clearly defined in this book and will guide and inspire anyone who desires to venture into this industry".

Pauline Parry
Author of the book: food | fun | love
President at Good Gracious! Events
www.goodgraciousevents.com

TABLE OF CONTENTS

ACKNOWLEDGMENTS

Once I finished writing this book, I realized that it was a task that I couldn't possibly have achieved on my own. There were a variety of wonderful people who helped me and supported my work in one way or another.

First, I'd like to thank my family who provided me with the time and space to complete what I now see as the beginning of my life's project. My wife Monica, my son Jorge, and my daughter Sandra were all incredibly patient during the endless hours that I spent writing. They are the greatest treasure that life has given me.

I would also like to thank my parents, Jorge and Lupita, and my siblings Rocio, Claudia, and Gerardo, for their tremendous love and support that has not only kept this family united, but also helped me remain strong.

Also thank you to T. Harv Eker and his staff at Peak Potentials for creating the wonderful educational programs that ultimately helped me change the course of my life at the right time.

I also want to give a big thank you to the people who have lead me, through their writings and teachings, on the adventure of finding and living my life purpose and embarking on this new and exciting endeavor of teaching what I know to the new generation of event planners. These people include Armand Morin, Ryan Lee, Mark Joyner, David Frey, Michel Fortin, Russell Bronson, and especially my friend and colleague Chris Farrell.

Finally, I'd like to thank all the people I have had the privilege to work with at my company SARAO, including my customers and co-workers. Without you, there would not be spectacular events to remember forever.

INTRODUCTION

EVENT PLANNING: AN EXCITING AND REWARDING CAREER

Event planning: it's an exciting and rapidly expanding industry, and one in which you can be extremely successful if you know how to go about it. There are lots and lots of event planners out there, but as with any other career or profession, the best and most skilled event planners enjoy the most profit and the most success.

And I know you want to fall into the successful category, right?

That's great to hear, because if that's what you want to achieve then you're in exactly the right place. Everything contained in this book comes directly from real world experiences, so you can be assured the information I'm providing here is legitimate and accurate.

I've already said that the event planning industry is expanding rapidly, and that is exactly right. One of the reasons for this is that an event planning business is low cost and low overhead to get started. Why? Because event planning is all about organizational skills, creative skills and planning skills, which all come directly from your brain. Everything else you need can be obtained from other sources.

These other sources can come from within an entire industry related to special event planning and event design. Examples include suppliers of different services like: caterers, audio visual companies, entertainment companies, and many others. There are also professional industry associations where event planners and their suppliers can come together for professional development, skill building, and most importantly, networking and connections.

For someone like you who wants to become an event planner, there has never been a better time to get started. The industry is growing, these kinds of services are in high demand, and the potential returns are high. If you truly decide to get into this business, I can tell you it is a promising and dynamic career, and one at which you can make a very nice living.

WHAT TO EXPECT FROM THIS BOOK

Let me begin by saying that the information contained in this book comes from my own personal experiences in building up my own event planning business. Because every situation is different, though, you will need to take the things I talk about here and adapt them to your own particular needs and circumstances. In other words, these are the things that have worked well for me, but if you want to make the most of your own business then you need to adjust them when necessary to make them work well for you.

So, what exactly can you expect to learn from this book? First and foremost, you are going to have access to insider information - the most valuable kind - showing you exactly how to go about setting up and developing your own successful event planning business. If you're willing to invest the time, energy, enthusiasm, and passion that is needed, then you can bring your dreams to life. You can own your own special event design and planning business.

FACT

As an entrepreneur and new business owner you must be prepared to put in a lot of hard work, face rejection from time to time, deal with setbacks, take some risks, and learn from your mistakes while building up your business.

What this book contains is the indispensable information I have gathered over my years as a special event planner, and it is all laid out in a format that's easy to read, easy to understand, and easy to use. It is **not** a magic formula, and you're not going to instantly be wildly successful; that would be a fairy tale and we all know fairy tales aren't real.

But with this book at your fingertips all of this will be substantially easier than if you were starting from scratch and learning it all on your own.

Think of it this way: if you decided you wanted to learn how to swim you would take swimming lessons from a professional instructor who would teach you step by step. You would still have to put in the effort to learn, and practice the steps taught to you by your instructor. But you would learn to swim, and you would become successful at it much faster than if you were trying to learn how to do it on your own without any idea how to go about it

That's exactly what this book is all about: teaching you the steps necessary to run a successful event planning business. With my information and your effort it is possible (and highly likely) to build a successful event planning business in a relatively short amount of time. You won't become a multi-millionaire overnight, and you won't go from start up to fully booked business in just a few weeks. What you will become, though, is a small business owner with the potential to be as successful as you want to become based on the amount of time, energy, and effort you want to put into the process.

Also, by all means, please remember to get some hands on work event planning before you start working with your first clients. This book is an excellent resource for those who are just getting started in the business and it indeed will teach you *most* of what you need to know. However, there is no substitute for real world experience! When I started my company, I had no knowledge or experience in business administration, marketing or sales, but I had a little experience in event planning.

There is nothing wrong with being new at special event planning, and everyone is new in the field at some point of time. However, being present at actual events can teach you things that you just can't comprehend from reading a book.

So how should you go about getting this experience? There is plenty that you can do when you are first starting out. For example, you can start by getting a job at a well established event planning business, or you could volunteer doing charitable event work. If you have children, why not help out with events at their school? Even helping to arrange birthday parties or weddings for your friends or relatives will prove to be useful experiences that will get you accustomed to planning special events. These type of experiences will prove to be invaluable when you actually get up and running with your own business. And who knows? You might even meet some great future clients in the process.

If you haven't already gathered, one of the main points that I am trying to make is that all entrepreneurs who are seeking to go into event planning need to get experience from the real world before embarking on their business adventures. Once you have read this book and also gotten some "dirt under your fingernails," you will be ready to launch a successful business.

HOW TO USE THIS BOOK

The best way to use this book is first to read it through from beginning to end. That way you will get a feel for the depth of information it contains and develop a better sense of just what it means to become an event planner. As you're reading, keep a notebook or spare pad of paper nearby for taking notes. Jot down any thoughts that come to you about what you're reading, including any questions, ideas, or observations. This process not only helps you to better understand the material as it's presented, but it also helps you to begin developing your own ideas and perspectives on just how your own special event planning business might take shape.

After your first pass through the content, go to the "Checklists and Resources" section at the end of the book and carefully review the checklists you need for getting started on your business. Work through each checklist carefully because doing so will help you tremendously and make it easier to avoid common mistakes and missteps. For each checklist, refer to the chapter where I go through the steps and the material in detail. This will also help you avoid common mistakes and allow you to focus on getting things "right" the first time around.

Finally, I strongly suggest you keep this book close by and easily accessible. Why? Because it contains such a wealth of information that you are likely to want to check back often to confirm information, look for new ideas, double check your progress, or just generally refresh your thoughts about a particular subject area. The chapters are laid out in a logical progression and each section is clearly labeled to help you quickly and easily find the information you need, whenever you need it.

ABOUT THE AUTHOR

You might be asking yourself, "Who is Jorge Zurita, and why should I read his book?" I know I would be asking that question if I were in your position, so let me finish this introduction chapter with some insight and explanation about myself.

When I launched my event planning and production business over 20 years ago, I had no knowledge or experience in business administration, marketing, or sales. In fact, it all started as a hobby of sorts at a time when very often I found myself short of money. Even the simple things, like taking my girlfriend to the movies, were difficult to afford, so I began looking for ways to earn some extra money.

As I was looking for earning ideas, I thought about how I used to organize all kinds of parties just for the sake of having fun. My parties became quite popular; in fact, and I fairly quickly developed a reputation for organizing really good and enjoyable parties. So I decided to turn my hobby into a business and I started offering my services as an event planning professional, specializing in theme parties. I only had $200 in my pocket and I used them to design a logo and print my first business cards.

I'd like to tell you about the moment when my business became seriously successful: the moment of truth for me. The first theme party that had great significance and a tremendous impact on my success during those early years was a tropical theme party. The success of this event had benefits for me long after the party was over and everything had been wrapped up.

I thought of throwing this party solely with the intention of making money. I charged an entrance fee, and got sponsorship products and money from different brands of beverages used and promoted during the event, including the number one global brand at the time. The number one Brazilian airline of the time was also a major sponsor. The idea of creating an event with a tropical theme was very exotic and appealing, since back in those days not many people of my age dared to go to places where tropical rhythms of all kinds, from Cuban salsa to Brazilian batucada, were played. If young people wanted to go out, they would go to the type of club that was traditional in the early 90's, so I saw the potential for my event to appeal to a large group of young people who wanted to experience something different.

At that time, I was studying my law degree at university, and I decided to promote my event to all the students at my university and at other institutions in the area. To attract them, I knew I had to have something that would generate interest in the party; something to spread the word that was both effective, and affordable for me.

After researching all the possibilities, I had an idea that changed the entire course of my business' destiny: I decided to give away a promotional piece for the event that also functioned as its exclusive invitation. I chose a very typical type of handcraft in Mexico, a maraca. I had them hand-painted with all the basic information about the event such as the location and the tropical dress code, in vibrant colors. I told people that if they did not come with their invitation – the maraca – they would not be able to get into the event.

I decided to name the party "Carnaval Tropical," and I used the slogan "La mejor fiesta del año" – the best party of the year. Choosing this catchy name for the festival and the accompanying slogan allowed me to continue to hold the event for another three years, having built the brand recognition with the successful first event. Every time I held the event more and more people were eager to come, not wanting to miss "the best party of the year."

Such a grand event needed many vendors and suppliers. I hired the venue, a caterer for hors d'oeuvres, several musical groups, a batucada band and some beautiful samba dancers, audio-visual equipment, lighting, and more. I struck deals with the suppliers to pay them in full once the event was over, since I planned to pay them with the proceeds from the entry charge. Can you imagine the risk I took? What if the event didn't work out as planned, or the theme did not appeal to people and no one showed up?

On the day, everything was arranged beautifully. I was impressed with the look and feel of what was, after all, my first fully-conceived theme party event ever. I'm not going to go into detail on how the party went, suffice it to say that it was one of my best events ever, and I received many comments of admiration and accolades. It felt great.

The thing that made all the different to the event, and the subsequent success of my business, was that maraca. I paid for the maracas upfront, as well as other items that were used as both promotional giveaways and contributed to the atmosphere of the party, such as hats, whistles and leis, and believe me when I tell you that this was the only cost I incurred.

The risk I took in negotiating with the suppliers to pay them after the event paid off, and my reputation went through the roof. Not long after the event took place, my telephone started to ring from people who had attended the party or heard of it, asking if I could possibly do an event like that for them.

It would not be stretching the truth to say that the success of my business ultimately comes down to a hand-painted maraca. What will the moment of truth be for your business?

Anyway, on with my tale. My very first client gave me a down payment of less than $600 which I used as an initial investment in the startup of my business. For that particular event I hired out everything I needed, using third party suppliers who agreed to wait until after the actual event to receive payment for their services. The event itself was a huge hit, the client was ecstatic, the suppliers were happy to get paid, and I was, quite frankly, hooked. Being an event planner seemed like the perfect fit for me and for my future.

So despite being in the precarious situation of having little to no startup capital, I moved forward anyway. I launched my event planning business and focused all of my energy and attention on making it a success. And in just eight short years, my company became one of the most recognized and successful event management companies around. Clients actively sought me out for a whole range of event planning needs, from corporate themed events to integration activities such as team building, and more. Today my clients include many Fortune 500 level companies, professional associations, institutions and private individuals.

Now, it should be obvious looking back on my first client event that the $600 down payment and the profits I made from that event didn't go very far. I couldn't afford a fancy office or anything else like that, so I did all of the work from my living room. But from that first moment on I was on the path to earning more money and making a higher level of income than any of my friends at the time. Whether they were just starting out in the business world or had had stable employment for a while, my friends saw the success I was having and I felt very good about the direction my business was taking me.

PATH TO SUCCESS

Over the years, I built my business by using my imagination and creativity to explore the myriad possibilities of themed entertainment, taking it out side the box.

Today my company has grown and evolved to levels I never dreamed were possible during those early days. The success I have enjoyed and innovation I have used to create that success not only allowed me to build a terrific business, but also inspired me to write this book.

But writing this book was not my first impulse. No, my first thoughts were to expand my company and turn it into a franchise operation. What would make it different from so many other franchises was the fact that franchisees could have it up and running within just a 30-day time frame. I knew that a franchise system would work very well with my business model because while the specific reasons for my expansion and growth were numerous and varied, the answer was always the same when someone asked about the keys to my success:

- _Key #1_ - I created a bulletproof system to organize and operate innovative, fun, and unforgettable events.

- _Key #2_ - I always offer and deliver services and products in a unique and creative way that resonates with my clients' desires, wishes, and emotions.

I was certain my expertise could be used by other entrepreneurs (like you) so they, too, could expand their horizons and run their own event planning businesses. What's more, I knew these same entrepreneurs could easily distinguish themselves from the competition simply by using my innovative approaches, models, products, and services. The challenge was to figure out a way to take the business formula I had spent 20 years developing and put it into a practical and comprehensive package of information that prospective franchisees would be able to easily understand and use.

As I started working on this I tried to calculate the number of events I had planned throughout my career and the total man hours I had spent organizing and producing themed events, entertainment functions and integration activities, but the calculations quickly yielded numbers in the thousands. How could I take the huge volume of cumulative data, information, and knowledge, and condense it into an efficiently-structured course that any franchisee could learn and apply to have their own event planning business up and running in 30 days?

It felt and sounded like something close to impossible. But it was this exact challenge that got me fired up and enthusiastic. I wanted to place the emphasis on putting together all of that information in a comprehensive and intuitive manner so investors could get one of my franchises and start their event planning business in a snap. Although I had figured this task would be difficult, surprisingly, it was not, and now you'll find out why this was the case.

That's right, the task that I was dreading – putting all this information together in an efficiently-structured course – turned out not to be difficult at all. Why? Because by this point in my event planning career, I was so familiar with the industry and with the workings of my business, that I intuitively knew what I needed to tell franchisees and the information basically just poured out of me.

It wasn't long before the franchise model and package were complete. So I launched it in the marketplace, asking $25,000 as the initial franchise fee. I hoped for and expected a good response, but the response I received was nothing short of overwhelming. More people than I ever thought possible were expressing interest in opening an event planning business by acquiring my franchise.

I was, of course, thrilled at the response; I was hearing from lots of people who expressed their interest in starting their own special event planning business. They recognized that by using my franchise model, my brand and my one–on–one personal coaching, they could successfully build a business organizing special events, theme parties, and team-building events.

But there was one big drawback for the majority of those who contacted me: money. Due to the economic downturn and the financial challenges being felt literally all over the world, there were a lot of enthusiastic, qualified, energetic, and excited entrepreneurs who definitely had the potential to succeed but simply could not afford the initial franchise fee. I completely understood exactly where they were coming from. Remember, I had been there myself, with no more than $200 in my pocket and a big dream to succeed.

So, I took my newly created package for the franchise business and began to pare it down. I removed my company brand name, and all those boring-but-necessary legal documents, procedures and formalities that a franchise business agreement requires. I also subtracted other things included in the franchise model, like the use of our web-based software for quoting event services and managing operations, and ended up with a complete package of first-hand knowledge and information about how to start and run a profitable event planning business from home.

I called my product the Aways Great Events System, or AGE for short. Using this, I was able to reduce the cost of my knowledge package, in comparison with that of my original franchise model, while making sure that all the most valuable information was retained. Once I had removed all the franchise elements, I found that what I was left with was all the essential tools for starting up and succeeding in an event planning business.

After creating the Always Great Events System, I realized that there was still one more step that I needed to take. I realized that there would be some people who might not have the money to buy the Always Great Events System, despite its reduced cost. So for these people I decided to write this book, as an introduction to both event planning and to my system.

By reading this book you'll learn a tremendous amount about event planning and how to succeed at it, but I still believe that to give yourself the very best odds for success you should at some point consider purchasing my Always Great Events System or my franchise.

So now let me return to my original statement, "why should you read this book?"

The answer, quite simply, is for knowledge. I'm supplying you with the knowledge and expertise you need to succeed, and now all you need to supply is the motivation and energy necessary to make that success a reality. This book, along with the detailed information on my website, www. JorgeZurita.com, can help you to start your new event planning business from scratch. If you are already working in the event planning industry, this information will show you how to expand and improve your existing business to achieve dramatic levels of success.

Look, I'm not all that special. I'm just a guy who experienced success with a plan I dreamed up one day and turned into a life's project. However, I am confident that with the strategies presented in this book and the opportunity to access more extra information via my blog at www. JorgeZurita.com, you too can succeed on a grand scale.

I have succeeded beyond my wildest dreams, and I would love to know that I have helped you do the same.

Are you ready? Then let's get this party started!

CHAPTER 1

WHY BECOME AN EVENT PLANNER?

"The only place where success comes before work is in the dictionary."

-- Vince Lombardi, the greatest football coach of all time

THE REWARDS OF BEING AN EVENT PLANNER

If you want to be an event planner working from home, that's terrific.

Event planning is an excellent way to make money and have a very rewarding career. It is the kind of job that can give you the flexibility to create your own business while providing you with significant economic freedom. Whether you're at your home office taking care of all the details or in the field setting up an event, in this business every day is a party!

It's also the kind of business in which you will work with a wide variety of people and a diverse group of clients that you will find in few other fields. What's more, you'll have opportunities to develop your amazing creative potential by visualizing every aspect of an event long before it happens.

Yes, you will take on significant challenges at times, and often work long hours under pressure too—but when all is said and done, you will celebrate your success when you see the amazed faces of people being captivated and awed by the magic of an event you organized. And I promise you, the feeling you get is like nothing else in this world you have ever experienced.

Welcome to the magical, over-the-top, unexpected, fascinating, and fabulous world of the special event professionals!

If you take your own mission to succeed seriously, follow my program and adapt it to your own particular circumstances and needs, this can become one of the most rewarding choices you have ever made. If you choose to take advantage of my program, you will have the enviable task of helping families, businesses, and community organizations to plan and run events that allow them to:

- Commemorate milestones like birthdays or anniversaries

- Accomplish goals and exchange ideas by helping corporations get their people together

- Raise funds through galas, auctions, or benefits

- Celebrate holidays, appreciation days, and other special events

- Enjoy family gatherings such as reunions

- Celebrate new beginnings like weddings

As a special event planner, it will be your job to make these events memorable and fun for those participating and carefree for the individual or team who hired you.

BENEFITS OF OWNING YOUR OWN EVENT PLANNING BUSINESS

Because you are reading this book, you are taking an important first step along the path toward owning your special event planning business. I know you are very excited by your decision to investigate this wonderful opportunity further, but you are probably also a little bit scared, too. Believe me, this is absolutely normal and I totally understand how you feel because I have been there myself. When I started my business I too was really nervous and afraid of not having what it takes to succeed.

I know now that was nonsense.

Remember...

Planning and producing special events is not as easy as it may seem; it's a complex activity that requires careful attention to detail and attention to the objectives your client has set for the event itself.

Why? Because succeeding as a special event planning professional is not hard as long as you're committed to going about it the right way. And if I can be successful, doing it without having any previous knowledge about event planning, marketing, sales or any other aspect of starting, running and growing a business, I am positive that you can do it too.

One of the really great things I've discovered is that there are a lot of rewards to being self-employed in a solid, well-run home-based business. Event management and planning is an industry that hasn't slowed down for the 20 years I've been doing it, and every indication is that it will continue to grow. In fact, special events and parties are big business: the special event planning industry accounts for billions of dollars in annual spending in the United States and around the world. And if the amount of money that can potentially be made isn't enough to inspire you, consider this: it's a terrifically fun business to be in!

Some of the many benefits of owning your own special event planning and management business include:

- You determine your own work schedule.

- You work at your own pace each day.

- You report only to the best boss possible... yourself.

- You can set your schedule and be at home with your children if you are a mom or a dad.

- You can do other activities since you have more flexible time and manage your own agenda.

- You can spend more quality time with your family and friends.

- You can travel more often because you literally carry your office with you.

- You control your income through performance, effort and commitment to your work.

- You cannot be laid off.

- You can make a nice living.

- You can have lots and lots of fun – and attend a lot of great parties!

If you ask me, there's nothing better than working for yourself and doing what you truly love, and after talking with my friends and colleagues who once worked for someone else and now own their own businesses, I'm more convinced than ever that this is true; none of these people would ever want to trade roles again. Nobody with common sense will honestly believe that working for someone else is better than being self-employed and owning your own successful business.

Regardless of what type of an event provider you want to become, this book can help you put all the pieces together to get started with this amazing entrepreneurial adventure and experience the kind of success you want and deserve!

SELF-ASSESSMENT: IS THIS CAREER RIGHT FOR YOU?

If you are serious about becoming a special event planning professional, you really have to make sure this is the right business for you. Yes, you need to be completely and totally passionate about what you are doing, and yes, you have to be willing to work hard and have a tremendous customer service attitude. You also need to have the right mindset and always be programmed to seek success, no matter what.

The most common mistake I see is that people think that just because they are extremely creative and talented, they have what it takes to run their own successful special event planning business. While this is a positive mindset, running your own successful business doesn't really require these things. It doesn't really matter if you are a very creative and talented individual, or if you already work in special event planning at another company, or even if you love putting on parties and would like to turn it into your full time career. No, none of these things mean anything at all if you don't also have the strategies and skills necessary to actually run a business.

Why? Because turning your passion into a profitable business takes a lot more than bright ideas and a handful of creative skills, experience, and/or talent.

FACT:

The way you handle the _business_ side of your venture is the most critical of all; it is what can really make or break your business and means all the difference between being successful and being broke.

You have to have a business focus that's at least equal to (if not greater than) your creative focus. Remember, the creative side of you is what stands out when the outside world looks at what you're doing, but the business side of you, when you're calculating your profits and planning the best way to increase them moving forward, is what actually makes your business succeed.

Part of a solid business focus is being very aware of your strengths as well as your weaknesses; I would go so far as to say this awareness is of the utmost importance when it comes to the success (or failure) of your business.

If you...

- don't know and don't want to learn how to manage money and other resources wisely

- don't like being surrounded by people

- don't like to work longer hours

- are not an organized individual

- dislike to coordinate a lot of tasks simultaneously

... then special event planning may not be the right choice for you to make if you want to start your own business.

This is such an important and fundamental part of success that I pay very close attention to this issue in my coaching program, in which I provide my subscribers with a very simple yet extremely effective test to help them identify their personal characteristics and find out if they are likely to succeed in this business or not.

However, just because a weakness is identified, it does not mean you absolutely cannot be successful. On the contrary, I strongly believe that any weakness or lack of knowledge can be easily overcome if you have the right attitude, openness to learning and a strong sense of accountability.

As you continue reading through this book, you will see that the key to your success is a combination of two things: knowing whether or not this business is the right one for you, and applying the information I'm giving you about how to conduct this business the right way, the first time around.

I will even go so far as to say this will guarantee your success. By following the information and step-by-step advice contained in this book and presented on my continually updated blog , you can avoid the mistakes most people typically make when they launch a commercial activity or business for the first time. Oftentimes, the number one mistake people make is not choosing the right business for them, because they do not dig deep enough into themselves in the early stages in order to find out if they are choosing the right business from the start.

This is important to me in a very personal way because I remember how much money I wasted and how much stress I suffered by not knowing what to do - and what not to do - in this business. And this happened because I simply had not identified my many weaknesses; without knowing that information, it was challenging to figure out how to successfully manage this type of business.

Remember...

Knowledge is power and, by giving you the knowledge you need (about yourself as well as about event planning), this book will give you power to make a good decision and focus your energy on something that is truly productive for you.

Of course, I ended up succeeding because of my burning passion for special events; but, if I had had all the valuable information I'm about to reveal to you when I started, I am sure I would have invested much less time, much less heartache and much less money... and success would have come much more quickly.

In other words, I am giving you an opportunity to do a thorough self-assessment and clearly determine if this business is the right choice for you before you go any further along in the process.

LEARN FROM OTHERS AND AVOID COMMON MISTAKES

Fortunately, I learned from my mistakes and went on to be hugely successful. Today, not only do I run one of the most recognized special event and theme party planning firms in my country, Mexico, but I also have other partners running their own businesses on a franchise model that I sold them before launching my coaching program.

These franchise partners followed the same steps that I took that led me into owning a successful and recognized event planning business, and in today's world that is really saying something. Economically, times are tougher today than I can ever remember them being before. What's more, most people have no idea what business they want to start and, even if they do have a general idea of what they want to do, they have no idea where to start or where to go with their new business endeavor.

I talk with people all the time who are sick and tired of working for someone else, whether it's for a large corporation or a small business of some sort. They are not fulfilled by what they are doing and they take little pleasure or satisfaction from their daily activities. Even worse, they live under the constant threat of losing their job due not only to this bad economy, but also to the ever-changing times that we live in.

Everything you need to know about launching and running an event planning business from home is contained in these pages. You have already chosen to make an investment in this book. If you like what you find, then you'll be in an excellent position to move forward and go to the next level. You can choose to start your own special event planning business from home and, when the time is right, expand into the next level of leasing an office space or perhaps a studio space elsewhere. Whatever choice you make, you'll be moving in the right direction because you'll understand the vital importance of focusing your efforts, giving it everything you've got and boldly moving toward your ultimate goals in order to achieve true success.

Welcome to the special event planning profession. Let's get this party started!

If you would like more information on how to start and run your event planning business, join my insiders list at www. MasteringEventPlanning.com.

CHAPTER RECAP

1. Event planning can be an exciting and rewarding career, as well as an excellent way to make money. It can provide you with a great deal of flexibility and a very nice income.

2. Some of the benefits of owning your own event planning business include:
- Control over your work schedule
- You can work from just about anywhere you want
- You are in control of your income

3. Before launching into an event planning business, be sure to conduct a self-assessment to determine if it is the right career choice for you. Success in this profession requires both a strong _creative focus_ and a strong _business focus_.

4. The information in this book is designed to take you step by step through all of the necessary processes and activities to start your business and be successful as an event planner. If you follow the advice and information in this book, you greatly increase your chances of success.

5. Learn from others as much as possible so you can avoid making common mistakes and thus achieve success more quickly than if you were trying to do it all on your own.

CHAPTER 2

GETTING STARTED IN EVENT PLANNING

"A journey of a thousand miles must begin with a single step."

-- Lao Tzu, Chinese philosopher

THE BIG PICTURE: WHAT IS AN EVENT?

It always helps to know the terminology and jargon of the profession you're involved in and special event planning is no different. So let's begin then with a solid working definition of an event.

According to the Merriam-Webster dictionary, an event is "something that happens at a given place and time." This is an accurate definition, but is too simplistic for our purposes here. A more complete definition, based on my 20+ years of experience in the event planning business, is as follows:

"An event is something that happens at a given place and time, involving a group of people gathering for a common purpose such as celebration, recreation, or to establish a common communication code."

Building from this definition, I strongly believe that to launch a successful career in the world of event planning it is essential to have in-depth knowledge about the concepts and "big picture" ideas that govern this industry. This knowledge will help you distinguish events by their type and characteristics and thus put you in a much better position to plan and implement them effectively.

In-depth knowledge of these aspects of event planning and management will tell you, for example, whether a sporting event is an actual sports competition or just a marketing campaign to promote a brand of sports product; or, whether a dance event is an actual party or just a promotional event put on by a record label to gain exposure for their musical acts and/or products.

This depth of knowledge will also make it easier to identify the appropriate products and services to choose in order to solve the specific needs of the client and stay within your budget. Armed with this information about the big picture surrounding a particular type of event, you will more easily recognize which suppliers or vendors will cater to your needs, and the influence they have on the supply chain of services to reach the final client, your client. Thus it will be much easier for you to implement effective marketing strategies surrounding the event and your business itself.

To efficiently convey a message, it has been my experience that nothing in the world beats a "live" event whose focus is communicating a message in the fields of human relations, culture, marketing, public relations, politics, diplomacy, or social gatherings. Only at a live event will you truly interact with your message's recipient in a profound manner. You will establish a close rapport and discover the essential elements of understanding and properly dealing with your client's many necessities and concerns.

With this in mind then, it's easy to see why the study and mastery of an event's "big picture" is necessary to start and pursue a successful event planning career in whatever event category you choose within the industry.

COMMON TYPES OF EVENTS

In this section I will introduce the most common types of events we see in the professional event planning industry. This will help you identify more clearly the scope of your focus when launching your event planning business.

Important

Keep in mind that not all types of event will interest you for your purposes of doing business, but I believe it's important to point out their main characteristics so you can gain a clear understanding of each type.

Artistic and cultural events

These events are intended to provide a space to promote various forms of artistic expression and/or to disseminate culture. They focus on knowledge, traditions and customs of people, whether from all around the world, within a local community, from a particular country or region or the like. Examples of this type of event might include a book fair, an art exhibition, a film festival, a posthumous tribute to a writer, artist, or intellectual, or a cultural fair.

Institutional and political events

These events are planned to communicate specific ideas, and sometimes to spread propaganda about governmental actions, political issues, politicians, or institutional projects. They can also be used as a form of advertising and promotion for one or more members of a government, political organization or institution. These types of events are often funded by public money or institutions whose management is sometimes subject to such special legal and regulatory requirements, or they may be sponsored by political parties, NGOs, or international agencies. The intended audience for an institutional or political event can be quite varied and will depend on the underlying goals and purposes of the sponsoring organization. Examples of this type of event might include a multinational meeting to discuss global warming, or a campaign to support a particular political candidate or slate of candidates.

Corporate and private events

These types of events are organized by corporations, private individuals and other organizations for a wide variety of purposes. Because of this tremendous variety, I find them to be among the most interesting and exciting events of all for an event planning professional. Examples of this type of corporate event are numerous and include the following:

- Conferences

- Conventions

- Exhibitions

- Employee appreciation events

- Client appreciation events

- Fundraising, non-profit events

- Product launches

- Trade shows

- Product or service promotions

- Corporate picnics

Additional examples of this type of private event are also numerous and include the following:

- Weddings

- Bar mitzvahs

- Quinceañeras

- Sweet sixteens

- Birthday parties

- Anniversaries

- Family gatherings

- Family reunions

- Bachelor and bachelorette parties

- Baby showers

- Graduations

These types of event are critical because they are at the very heart of our business model as event planning professionals. It is these kinds of events that will likely make up the bulk of your business activities and bring in the majority of your revenue.

WHAT SERVICES DOES AN EVENT PLANNER PROVIDE?

The most common services provided by an event planner include the following areas:

DID YOU KNOW...

Traditionally, feasts and celebrations were typically held exclusively in "holiday" venues such as hotels, social clubs and homes. In today's marketplace, however, almost any venue or locale can be adapted to the needs of your client and used to throw a party or big event.

Venue research and selection

This service involves researching the best places available to meet your client's goals and objectives for their event, presenting them with these options, and then helping them to select the best venue for their needs. More and more companies and individuals using the services of a professional event planner today are seeking original or uncommon places in which to hold their events as well as creative and innovative ways to put them on, so the number of choices for alternative venues is expanding every day.

The most common examples and types of venue we use today include:

- Hotel ballrooms and/or special event rooms

- Restaurants

- Night clubs, bars, and pubs

- Museums

- Exhibition/convention centers

- Outdoor parks

- Theme parks

- Historic sites

- Tents and marquees

- Empty spaces such as parking lots, lofts or even warehouses

- Beaches and pools

- Gardens

- Roof gardens

- Country clubs

- Golf courses

- Schools

- Shopping malls

- Boutiques

- Galleries

- Public buildings

- Sports arenas

- Public areas

- Zoos

- Stage theaters

- Movie theaters

- Haciendas, ranches & farms

Ground and air transportation

This service involves researching prices listed for ground and air transportation options for the operation of the event, and then putting together a recommended package of transportation arrangements. Upon approval by the client, you are then responsible for coordinating all transportation logistics, up to and including:

- Shipments

- Cargo

- Personnel

- Entertainment

- Staff

Design, production, and assembly of themed environments

This service involves all aspects of putting together a themed environment, whether it is for an event, a party or some other activity of a theatrical nature. Most professional event planners will, at some point in their careers, definitely be involved in these kinds of events and the tasks associated with them.

Your role is to create the selected "atmosphere" for the event through use of a variety of tools and techniques, such as:

- Food

- Beverages

- Music

- Costumes

- Games

- Contests

- Artistic talent such as acrobats, dancers and jugglers

- Table dressings

- Centerpieces

- Party favors

- Flowers

- Lighting

By using these tools and techniques, you can create an environment where your client and their guests feel as if they have been "transported" to another time, place, or situation. Other aspects of this role can include locating and managing other players in the theme or drama you're trying to create, such as hosts/hostesses, singers, actors, musicians, and dancers.

Selecting and dealing with vendors and suppliers

This service involves guaranteeing that your client will save time and stress by selecting and dealing with the right team of vendors and suppliers to meet every single need for the event or activity. The client benefits from the ease and convenience of only having to deal with one person (you) to coordinate and deal with all of these things, while you benefit from being able to more fully control and effect the execution of the event by exerting control and influence over each of the vendors and suppliers.

BUSINESS TIP

It is important to use the services of several different vendors and suppliers across different events and activities; you are able to establish good working relationships and gain a better perspective on which suppliers are most appropriate for which situations.

The ideal event planning professional will always have access to more than one provider for every need, thus always having a backup available should a particular vendor or supplier fail to meet his or her needs in some way.

What's more, when your vendors and suppliers know you are actively using them and their competitors for your variety of events, they are far more likely to be focused on meeting (or exceeding) your expectations in order to win more of your business in the future. In other words, let them compete a bit for your business and you'll be in a better position to get them to meet your exacting needs for your events.

Some examples of the types of services, suppliers and vendors you'll need to have access to include the following:

- Catering

- Floral arrangements

- Tents, stages, and dance floors

- DJs

- Musical bands and folkloric groups

- Models and hostesses

- Waiters and catering staff

- MCs and animators

- Live entertainers

- Coordinating staff

- Security personnel and systems

- Registry control

- Language interpreters

- Valet parking

You will likely find specialists in some or all of these areas, which can offer you distinct advantages, such as knowing that the chosen vendor will be an expert in that particular area. The potential disadvantage of using too many specialist vendors, however, is that you increase the number of different suppliers you're coordinating with throughout the event planning and execution. It's a good idea then, to strike a balance between securing the most expert specialty suppliers and vendors you can, while trying to minimize the number of different vendors or suppliers you have to deal with throughout the event.

When you are dealing with vendors and/or suppliers, always remember to be highly ethical. Make sure that you treat these business people like partners and seek to coordinate a win-win relationship. When you treat these people kindly and with respect, they will want to work with you on future occasions.

CRITICAL SKILLS TO BE A SUCCESSFUL EVENT PLANNER

As with any profession or career, you will need certain skills to be a successful event planner. These include, but are not limited to, the following:

- High energy level

- Able to withstand long working hours

- Able to tolerate a high level of stress

- Excellent leadership qualities

- Highly organized

- Able to manage money wisely

- Highly systematic

- Outstanding communication and interpersonal skills

- Outstanding oral and written communication

- Able to make decisions effectively and efficiently

- Be respectful of all parties involved

Perhaps you're wondering why some of these qualities are even on this list, so let's look at them in a bit more detail.

FACT:

Your job is to efficiently orchestrate the work of many specialists and make things happen in one place and time in order to achieve a successful outcome.

As an event planner, you need to be an excellent leader, as you'll be responsible for coordinating the activities and tasks of all members of your staff whether they are your own employees or employees of one of your vendors or suppliers.

You also have to be organized, because as an event planning professional you must simultaneously juggle large amounts of information flowing in from and out to each client and relating to each particular contract. It can become so overwhelming and difficult sometimes that it might seem impossible to manage; even worse, a single error or omission in communications between your client and/or a supplier can be devastating to the outcome of the event itself. This is why it is so critical to be highly organized and learn how to systematically manage all of that information and store it for easy access. It is in this way that you will be best able to stay on top of things and have the ability to serve your clients in an expeditious and professional manner.

In my own event planning business, I use a very efficient Internet-based system that allows me to store all of my clients' information, history, contact details, previous events and incoming and outgoing e-mails, as well as most of my operating documents. It also allows me to upload all of the products and services I can offer to a central point, complete with a description, price, attributes, cost, discounts, commissions, taxes and even a photo of each item where applicable, so I can create quotes very easily and fast.

CONTINUAL LEARNING AND IMPROVEMENT

If you want to be an event planner, you must be well informed about industry trends and be willing to constantly be in a state of learning about different cultural topics, technology, marketing and public relations. This, in turn, means you have to want to develop an ever-creative mind with an intense focus on continual learning and professional improvement.

There are a number of key elements and skills you have to learn and constantly work to improve if you are serious about succeeding in this career. Here are some top tips for doing this most effectively:

**Tip #1** - I strongly recommend you search for and subscribe to some of the many online newsletters about event planning, and also join Internet forums on the event planning topics that interest you the most. This will keep you well informed and will reinforce your position as an expert, since you'll be able to manage updated information and make suggestions based on that information. This will result in your clients seeing you as a valuable asset to bring their event into reality because they will feel they are in good hands. Remember, if you are going to claim to be an expert in event planning, be it social gatherings, corporate conventions, themed parties or anything else, you had better be very well-versed on topics such as different cultures, marketing, public relations and technology marketing, public relations and technology

For example, let's say a corporation comes to you asking for advice and services to develop a strategy for delivering a commercial or promotional message to a certain audience through an event. You must be able to understand and feel as comfortable talking about marketing concepts and principles as you do about making suggestions and offering comments on the different resources available in the market that multimedia technology has to offer. Additionally, you need to have demonstrable expertise in the plethora of sophisticated communications tools and devices available that will make the communication process more interactive and efficient at an event.

Tip #2 - It's also very important to be knowledgeable about different cultural topics; this is especially true if you are offering your services as a professional planner of themed events. So if a client comes to you asking you to develop a custom theme party according to their very specific needs or ideas (i.e., a sophisticated "Surrealistic Art Soirée," a Hawaiian luau, or an Art Deco Awards Night) you must be able to understand and talk about each concept at least at a basic level. If you cannot do so, then chances are you are not going to engage your prospective client emotionally, and your sales arguments and ideas are not going to resonate at all with him or her.

In my case, I stay culturally informed by constantly trying to learn from every possible resource or channel of information within my reach that is related to the subject at hand. For example, if I go to the movies to watch an historic film, I pay attention to the environment in each scene so I can learn more about architecture, interior designs, music styles and fashion from that era. Or, if I have a little spare time, I visit a local bookstore and go directly to the design, art, architectural, and illustrated books to read about every imaginable subject under the sun.

Additionally, I make a point of regularly reading about corporate business matters so I can speak and understand the same language as my corporate clients do. Or, if I'm traveling and have a little extra time in a particular town or city, I go to local arts-and-crafts stores and local museums to learn as much as possible about that particular culture. By doing these things on a regular and consistent basis, when the opportunity arises to talk about these subjects I can feel comfortable speaking about that culture or style in a very genuine and well informed manner while holding a simple conversation.

MORE CRITICAL SKILLS FOR SUCCESS

As an event planner, you have to be highly responsible, always willing to put in extra effort and capable of sharing risks and making decisions quickly and accurately. You have to be able to work both day and evening events and not be afraid of devoting many extra hours of time in order to create memorable events for your clients. You must also be a good salesperson and have adequate knowledge of public relations, as well as an ability and willingness to learn more about these disciplines on a regular basis. In this way, you will stay well informed and continuously improve on the skills necessary to master the rules of social, business, and interpersonal relationships.

Additionally, every time that you plan an event, it is important to give it your 100%. Even if it isn't a particularly important day for you, your clients will be relying on you for some of their most precious memories. Give everything that you can to your clients and really listen to their needs.

Further, when you are running your own business, you are responsible for your client's satisfaction. They will also be putting a good deal of trust in you. Therefore, it is essential to always give them a high quality product. Never charge them outrageously high prices, as it is important to deal fairly with each client.

If you plan to organize special events, theme parties, and team building activities, you have to develop an active and creative mind. This means always being able to come up with original and appealing ideas that captivate the attention of your clients and that resonate with them personally or professionally. Stay on top of new trends so that you can give clients the most cutting-edge advice and guidance possible. You had better also have a good sense of humor, enjoy being around and getting to know other people, and know how to have fun at an event. When you have these qualities and let them shine you will ensure that your clients and their guests will have a great time at your events.

FACT:

Written documents are the face of your business when you are not there representing your business in person. It makes sense then for those documents to represent your business just as professionally and effectively as you do in person.

This is why I am constantly reminding myself of the following:

If I have fun and enjoy the process of creating and running an event, chances are my clients and their guests will also enjoy it and have fun.

Two other critically important skills to develop if you want to be a successful event planning entrepreneur are copywriting and using good grammar. Why? Every written document that leaves your business is a reflection on your business so it must read well, be accurate, and look professional.

It is also critical to be as clear and specific as possible when communicating ideas, which requires high-level writing skills. These skills not only allow you to communicate clearly and concisely, they also demonstrate to your clients that you pay close attention to detail and specifics. This will make them more confident that you will also pay close attention to the details and specifics of their particular needs and objectives.

On the other hand, if you can't communicate in a clear and coherent manner in your writing, then chances are your clients will not be confident you have the ability to meet the needs and objectives of their planned event. The result is that you probably will not get the job at all and the client will turn to someone else for event planning services.

Consequently, I strongly recommend you work to improve your writing and grammar skills regularly and continuously. You have no idea just how much this one simple yet vital skill will help you when it comes to closing deals and clarifying the path you have to follow to get a successful outcome on every project you take on.

Last but not least is your ability to use electronic tools and technology, such as the Internet, e-mail, databases, word processing programs, Excel and Power Point. Since you are already reading this book, I assume you already have a good grasp of these digital tools; if, however, you feel your skills are lacking in any of these tools, then I strongly recommend you make the effort to improve them.

FIND YOUR EVENT PLANNING NICHE

The bottom line for being a successful event planning professional is that you have to go where the money is, and with the Internet at your fingertips it is easier than ever to find out what services are most in demand. For all of the work and effort that goes into starting and building your business, you want to make sure the results and rewards you receive are in line with the effort you have put in.

In other words, if you are struggling away in a low-demand niche for professional event planners, you're going to have to work that much harder just to win the few clients there are out there looking for services such as yours. On the other hand, if you focus your efforts on a high-demand niche for professional event planners, you're going to have a much easier time attracting clients and winning the competition to plan and execute their events.

KEY CONCEPT FOR SUCCESS

With all of the tools available today for researching and evaluating potential niche markets, there is really no excuse for not having a good and accurate assessment of the potential market for the niche you are considering for your event planning business. Just a bit of time and effort put into this process up front will pay you huge dividends on the back end as you will be better able to focus your efforts on pursuing the kind of in-demand events that will keep your business busy and the revenues rolling in regularly.

If you follow the advice I'm giving you here, you will spare yourself a great deal of frustration and stress because it will keep you from embarking on a business that you either don't like or that doesn't have a lot of potential for generating a profit. The most important first step then is to start by clarifying what it is that you like or would like to do. Failure to do this right up front will almost certainly lead to failure further down the road, even if the area you choose to pursue is a profitable one. No matter how much money there is to be made in a particular area of focus, if it is an area you don't enjoy or you even really hate, then you're not going to be successful in the long run.

It's a cliché, to be sure, but it's mostly true:

Do what you love and the money will follow.

I say it's mostly true because it is also critically important not to consider any niche or area for which there isn't a potential and active market, regardless of whether you really like that particular thing. Again, you have to go where the money is. Whatever you decide to do as an entrepreneur will work best if a) it is something that many people actually need, are looking for and are willing to pay for, and b) if it is something that you really enjoy doing.

You also have to place yourself in a market where the product or service is bought more than once every year, otherwise your business could be in danger of never actually getting off the ground. For example, you wouldn't want to specialize in running Christmas-themed events because those would only be in high demand during a very short period of time each year. A better approach would be to specialize in major holiday-themed events (Thanksgiving, Christmas, St. Patrick's Day, Easter, May Day, Memorial Day, Independence Day, Labor Day, Halloween, Veteran's Day) that are in demand throughout the year.

So, I would suggest you take the following steps:

1. Make a list of the things that interest you. Review your current and past hobbies and be perfectly clear about what it is that you really enjoy the most or despise the most. Use this information and personal insight to evaluate options and see if you can turn that passion or hobby of yours into a viable event planning business.

2. Research similar businesses. Use every avenue available to you, such as the Internet, printed magazines, online magazines, newspapers, books, and every other means you can think of. The goal is to discover more about that specific activity that interests you and then see if there's actually a market for it. If there is, identify potential competitors and determine what it is that you can offer potential clients that they cannot or will not offer.

3. Check out blogs and other social networking sites. These are extremely useful for identifying which event planning activities are "hot" and "trendy" in your area. Make online friends and bounce ideas off them. Be an active participant in appropriate forums and discussion groups.

4. Use Google keyword tools. Use these free and extremely powerful tools to scan and measure keywords in order to find out if there are people out there searching for the particular service you're thinking about offering.

Remember, the more energy you spend on clarifying and identifying the most specific details of what it will take to move forward in your chosen event planning niche, the more likely it is you will be successful. And one of the really great by-products of being successful is that you will be much more likely to truly enjoy being in the event planning business, despite the inevitable hassles, stresses and occasional setbacks you will encounter.

Use the information you collect to calculate your service rates to see if you can outbid existing competitors. Figure out ways to innovate and improve the services you offer in order to make your business stand out from the competitors. Do these things before embarking on your specific business activity and you will dramatically improve your chances of long term success.

And if you only pay attention to one thing I have written here, let it be this:

... if you are planning on specializing in one or more of the most typical event services listed above, and don't find any competitors or other companies related to your product or service business idea;

... if there are no books, magazines, Internet forums or other companies announced in the web or any other media selling what you are planning to sell;

... if there are no individuals already doing the same activities in your community;

DON'T EMBARK ON THAT PARTICULAR BUSINESS ACTIVITY!

If you do, then chances are you're going to be very disappointed or even worse, end up broke, because it could only mean one thing: there's no market for your business idea.

Pay attention to what other people are already doing and learn about hidden problems if you want to become truly successful.

COMMON MISTAKES TO AVOID

I talked earlier about the importance of avoiding the most common mistakes in order to increase your chances of success. That is, after all, why I wrote this book. I want to help you avoid the mistakes I made and use what I've learned over the last 20+ years to make your path to event planning success smoother, easier, faster and more enjoyable.

For that reason, I'm going to close this chapter with a list (shown in no specific order) of the most common mistakes to avoid as you contemplate moving forward with your professional event planning business:

- Don't go into business if you don't know as much as possible about what you are doing.

- Don't go into business with a partner; it is too difficult and most of the time it doesn't work.

- Don't go into business if you don't have the time it takes to make it grow or to update your knowledge about your new business.

- Don't let shyness hold you back; if you are a naturally shy person, set that aside and let it go. Instead, tell everybody about your new business and engage people in conversation about it whenever and wherever possible.

- Don't over promise when selling your services, but in every case always over deliver.

- Don't just price your services without researching the market for that particular service.

- Don't go into business without knowing what you want to accomplish and how you are going to do so.

- Don't try to sell your services as they are; try to adapt them to your client's needs.

- Don't say "yes" to everything your clients ask; take on only the jobs related to your area of expertise and, in cases where you must decline a request, kindly explain the reasons why you are doing so.

- Don't believe you can do everything, because you can't. Ask for help when you need it, and remember that you need it at any time when you are not totally sure you are going to deliver 100% of what you promised and/or 100% of what your client expects from you.

- Don't forget about your ethics. Ethics mean concern for the well-being of others, trustworthiness and honesty. You want to always represent yourself and your services fairly to your clients and partners. It is also essential never take advantage of anyone.

- Make sure that you have some real world experience before embarking in planning your first special events. After all this is a profession in the whole sense of the word, and you must agree that no one wants to go to the surgeon who has never lifted a knife before! With that idea in mind, make sure that you have gotten your hands dirty in some way, whether that means working for a while for another event planning business, volunteering with other people's events or working to help friends or relatives plan weddings or baby showers. The bottom line is that you need to have some real world experience before taking on your first clients.

With all of this said and after everything you've read so far, are you ready to start your event planning business?

If you have been honest in evaluating your talents and abilities in light of everything contained in this chapter and your answer is an enthusiastic "Yes," then you are ready to move on to the next steps.

Also, to keep learning about this particular topic and to discover the mistakes you must avoid when selling your event services, be sure to join my insiders list at www. MasteringEventPlanning.com.

CHAPTER RECAP

1. Take time to understand the definition of an event and develop the in-depth knowledge necessary to succeed in this industry. Pay particular attention to learning how to identify the right products and services to use in order to meet the needs of your clients while staying within their allotted budget.

2. As you consider which type of event planning you want to focus on, think about the most common types of events you might encounter in this industry:
- Artistic and cultural events
- Institutional and political events
- Corporate and private events

3. Event planners provide a number of different services, including:
- Venue research and selection

- Ground and air transportation
- Design, production, and assembly of themed events
- Selection of and dealing with vendors and suppliers

4. A successful event planner possesses a number of critical skills, such as:
- High energy level
- Ability to work long hours and tolerate high levels of stress
- Excellent leadership
- Highly organized and systematic
- Outstanding communication (oral and written) and interpersonal skills
- Efficient and effective decision-making

5. To achieve the greatest level of success, be fully committed to continual learning and improvement to develop your skills and professional abilities. Additionally, you must be willing to adapt to changing technology and find ways to continually serve your clients in ways that exceed their expectations.

6. Finding your particular event planning niche is a vital part of creating a successful event planning business. This will help you focus your efforts and hone in on the area in which you have the potential to make the most money over the long run. You can find your niche by doing a number of things, such as:
- Making a list of the things that interest you
- Researching similar businesses to evaluate the marketplace
- Checking out blogs and social networking sites

- Using Google keyword tools to evaluate demand

7. Review the common mistakes to avoid as presented in this chapter and use this information to help you move forward in a constructive manner.

CHAPTER 3

THE TRUTH ABOUT OWNING A HOME-BASED BUSINESS

"Even if you're in the right track, you'll get run over if you just sit there"

-- Will Rogers, Comedian

WORKING FROM HOME: CHANGES, CHALLENGES, AND REWARDS

I am going to address a lot of issues in this book in general terms and offer suggestions that worked for me and might work for you too. However, I'm not actually going to offer a pure step-by-step process on how to do each individual point of discussion; if I did that, I would either never finish this book or it would be a few thousand pages long.

The reality is that if you want to be a successful event planning entrepreneur, you have to get your hands dirty and find out how to do a lot of things by yourself. There are countless situations in which you have to be a proactive and clever problem solver; along the way you will also become a master of improvising outstanding solutions to any number of problems.

Now that you have decided to start a home-based business, your life, work environment, and how you spend your time will change dramatically. For instance, with a conventional job someone else set your hours, dictated your performance goals, and often even assigned you specific work tasks. As an entrepreneur and business owner though, all of a sudden you have plenty of things to think about and do, most of which will seem completely foreign (particularly because you are 100% in control of everything). Consequently, you must, without exception, develop a simple plan that will assist you in organizing the business operation.

Profitability and success in any business do not magically happen, and that is certainly true of professional event planning. It will take time and energy for you to adjust your focus and activities, and turn your business from a mere dream into a stable, profitable and solid reality. It's important to expect everything to seem more difficult in the beginning, and you may even feel that everything's evolving at a slower pace than you originally anticipated.

This is perfectly normal and to be expected.

The most important lesson for you to learn here is not to stop and quit when things become difficult, but rather to make the commitment to take the first step and the next step and the step after that; keep going, no matter what. You have to move on, move forward and get your hands a little bit dirty along the way.

For people undertaking these steps for the first time, I strongly suggest you think about and come up with answers to the following:

- Do you want to do this business on a full-time or part-time basis?

- How will you keep yourself updated and stay on top of the specific activity you have chosen to undertake in order to succeed overall in the event planning industry?

- What is your marketing strategy?

- What will you name your business?

- How will you design a logo and obtain printed materials to promote your services?

- How will you design and launch your web page?

- How will you identify the best vendors and build your commercial alliances to economize and get the best deals for your clients?

- How might your closest friends and family be able to help spread the word about your new venture to people they know?

- How will you most effectively invest your time and money in getting your business noticed, remembering that the name of the game here is "exposure" and that the more you expose your business to potential customers, the better the chances of getting more contracts?

With these thoughts and answers in hand, you're ready to move on to the three key steps necessary to get your home-based business up and running successfully.

STEP 1: SET UP YOUR WORKSPACE

FACT:

It's important to get out of your comfort zone as soon as possible and start arranging a new work space in your home so you can start working sooner rather than later.

The first and most obvious place to start, and the first major commitment you'll make to your home-based business, is to identify a suitable workspace in your home and convert that living space to accommodate the business operation. The second (and less obvious) task to accomplish is to start a "buzz" about your new business by spreading the word to acquaintances, family and close friends. This process allows you to let the reality of your decision "sink in" and sets the stage for moving forward with your actual business operations.

Regardless of whether you plan to work your business full-time or part-time, you will need privacy so that you can concentrate and focus on the tasks at hand. For most people this means setting aside space that will be dedicated exclusively to the business; in other words, space that is set aside from the hustle and bustle of the rest of your own daily life. This self-imposed isolation will allow you to clear your mind and focus on what needs to be done every day, as well as get yourself into the mindset that when you enter that space it's time to work.

But what if you don't think it's a good idea to work from home? Or maybe your home does not have enough room to accommodate a working space? I have found it good to go ahead and do whatever it takes to set aside a space (no matter how small) anyway. Try using portable dividers to separate a portion of your living room or dining room, or re-arrange the furniture a bit to create a semi-walled off area in which to work.

By doing this you will save yourself the expenses of rent, utilities, and parking at an outside office space, a very im-portant issue during the startup phase when money is ex-ceptionally tight. Resist the urge to move on to another location right away; wait until you feel comfortable with the amount of revenue your business is bringing in and making the investment to move on to the next level, outside office space.

Now that you've set aside your work space, what do you put in it? This is where you have to start thinking out of the box because it's far too easy to quickly spend a whole lot of money setting up an office with every supply, machine, device, and technology you can think of. It's far better to come up with a list of the most basic items to consider and then decide which ones to obtain based on your available money and where you think you'll get the biggest "bang" for your buck.

Here are the basic items I recommend considering:

Office equipment - Computer, cell phone (PDA prefer-ably), desk, chair, printer/fax/scanner, file cabinet, lamp, or other lighting.

Office supplies - White board, calendar, pens, paper, stapler, paper clips, file folders

Computer software - Word processor, spreadsheets, presentations

Separate business telephone line

Obviously, you're going to need some seed money to start your event planning business; it is an oft-repeated myth that you can start with zero money at all. Even if you don't have a whole lot of money, you do have many different options to consider and chances are you can be very creative about deciding how to come up with the necessary funds for start-up costs. You can use your savings, apply for a bank loan, approach friends to invest some money, have someone else help with your bills or, as a last resort, use your credit cards.

When dealing with office furniture, don't shoot for the moon and think "new is best," but instead opt for gently-used office furniture. It's available at consignment stores and used stores for a fraction of what it costs new, and it will be just as functional for your start up needs. Another option is to take that old table you inherited from your grandparents and turn it into your desk. Also, search through your garage; I guarantee you will find things you can use in the beginning, such as chairs, lamps, shelves, and other items to repurpose as office furniture.

Instead of buying a brand new computer, take your old one and give it a tune-up to be more compatible with your business today. Often, simply performing a maintenance service on your computer and increasing the size of the hard drive is enough to get you the functionality you need for a cost far less than buying an entirely new computer.

As for a printer, I strongly recommend getting an all-in-one model with print/fax/scan/copy functions together in one single device. You don't have to buy a top-of-the-line model either; head down to your local Wal-Mart, Costco, or Sam's Club and you can find an assortment of perfectly functional all-in-one machines for a very reasonable amount of money, or you can also catch a very good sale. Remember too, that technology like this is changing at a dramatic and rapid pace; what is state-of-the-art now will be bottom-of-the-line in just a few short months, so don't waste your money by buying equipment that is too expensive, especially in the beginning.

Regardless of how you decide to establish your own workspace, make it comfortable for yourself. One of the areas where I recommend spending a bit of extra money if you can afford it is on a sturdy, comfortable office desk chair. You're going to be spending a fair amount of time sitting and working in your new work space, so it's well worth it to indulge in a chair that will offer the support and comfort you need to put in the necessary long hours. I cannot emphasize enough how important your personal comfort will be, particularly when times get tough, busy or a particular job becomes stressful.

Consider too, adding in a picture or two to make your work space more comfortable, personal, and pleasant. Put up a colorful poster, place a picture of your family on the desk or have a mouse pad made with a picture of your favorite pet on it. These little touches, although inexpensive and easy to do, will help turn your office into your retreat and your think tank.

Congratulations, you now have your work space all set up. What's next?

STEP 2: DON'T PANIC

"Oh my God, what have I done?" is the most common question you will ask yourself once your office space is in front of your eyes. I like to think of it as the entrepreneurial version of buyer's remorse.

My friend, I can honestly tell you that I have been there many, many times since I started this business. In fact, every time I embark on something new I end up at some point having this predictable (but no less uncomfortable) moment of sheer terror. Even after going through this at least a dozen or more times, I can tell you it is still scary, it is still worrisome, and it is still a very necessary part of moving forward with your own business.

Look, a little panic is really a good thing because it is a powerful motivator to get out there and do what it takes to get your business up and running successfully. Just keep reminding yourself that you are your own boss and you are in total control of your financial destiny; I guarantee this will scare the heck out of you and stoke the fires necessary to take control and make things happen.

Also, keep in mind that you have one thing that I did not have, and that is knowledge. I have been through this process before and I've written this book specifically to pass along my hard-earned knowledge and help you be successful without having to make all of the common mistakes I made along the way.

Think of me as your invisible mentor.

I know, you're thinking to yourself, "Is this really supposed to ease my mind?!" The answer is yes, it is, because my guidance and advice will emphasize to you the critical importance of staying focused, continuing to press forward, and always, always keeping your eyes keenly focused on your goals. Why? Because it is this intensity and this commitment that will propel you through the difficult early times and help you get onto the track of becoming successful and prosperous.

FACT:

Without exception, it will take more than just a few weeks or even a few months to feel as if you are actually making positive progress toward your business goals. Sometimes it even takes longer periods of nonstop hard work to see tangible results.

STEP 3: REALITY CHECK

The most important thing to realize is that you can't expect to make much income very soon. In other words, don't start your event planning business with the expectation of bringing in a hefty amount of income right away. Even the most successful businesses seldom generate regular income in the beginning, and your event planning business is not likely to be the exception to this general rule. When you start this business, do it with the clear knowledge and expectation that it's going to take time for it to pay off, so please, be prepared for that fact and you'll avoid unpleasant surprises as well as unnecessary extra stress and worries.

With this in mind, it should be clear and easy to understand that nothing is more important than doing whatever it takes to start producing income. Anything you do that is aimed at anything besides making money, or undertaking any activities that do not lead to making money, is a waste of time in the early stages of your business. What you need in the beginning is a laser-like focus on applying your time and energy to those things that are going to produce income as soon as possible.

Of course, there will be some things that you'll need to do that do not relate or direct you to making a sale, such as planning and strategizing. However, watch out for those things that seem at first blush to be good uses of your time but in reality are more distraction than anything else.

Examples of these time-killers include things like:

- Going over your to-do list repeatedly

- Designing and re-designing your logo several times

- Naming and re-naming your business several times

- Endlessly tinkering with and perfecting your website

- Arranging and re-arranging your work space

- Setting up your telephone speed dial list

- Establishing and tinkering with your filing system

Yes, these are all important activities, but be honest with yourself about how much time you should truly be spending on them. Focus your time and energy on real, income-producing work rather than on excessive planning, revising, strategizing, or organizing.

All of the time you're tempted to spend on time-killers (or more accurately, income-production-killers) should instead be spent on making sales. Be honest and recognize how much of your time is spent on real income-producing work and how much of it is spent merely planning how you are going to produce it.

I'm not trying to dampen your enthusiasm, but I do want you to be fully prepared for the unexpected, frustrating, and time-consuming situations that you're bound to encounter when starting your event planning business. The fact is that you can successfully overcome most obstacles if you budget your startup expenses properly and have the right mindset, which means being prepared to face the unexpected and deal with challenges in a positive and direct manner.

Another area to watch out for is analysis; more specifically, beware of analysis paralysis. What does this mean? It means that if you spend too much time analyzing things you're going to end up paralyzing yourself and choking off the action and direction you need to be successful.

Now, earlier in this book I talked about the importance of getting a plan in place and establishing a clear strategy for how you will start this business running instead of simply walking. I stand by this advice because, in my experience, having a solid plan is critical to success; however, spending too much time, energy, and effort on creating a detailed, comprehensive business plan is a prime example of over-analysis.

A conventional business plan is really not necessary in the beginning, unless, of course, you are planning to borrow a lot of money from a traditional bank. In this situation they will almost certainly require you to provide them with a detailed business plan before they will even consider lending you any money.

As a general rule, you're much better off opting for a general plan of action (emphasis on the "action" part) that's practical, effective and easy to follow. You don't need to hire a consultant to write it for you; simply sit down, think about what you want to accomplish and set out a clear, concise path or strategy to follow on a daily basis in order to reach your end goals. This last piece is crucial; you must be very, very clear on your goals and ensure that they are attainable, accountable goals that you can achieve within a logical and realistic time frame.

You might still be asking yourself though, how do I actually go about doing that?

All you have to do is answer these questions and put everything in writing:

- What type of service or product do you provide in the event planning industry? Define it as clearly as possible.

- Who is your ideal client? Establish a profile for each one.

- How are your clients going to find out about you? Establish marketing strategies: newspaper ads, website, word of mouth, etc.

- Is there a market for your services? Identify and check the competition, whether your targeted potential clients are already buying their services and, if possible, what prices they are paying.

- What sets you apart from the competition? Price, quality of service, general expertise, location, creativity, specialization, etc.

- What are your costs?

- What are your prices?

- What are your income expectations vs. needs? Be realistic about how much you want to make at any point in time versus what you need to make at any point in time.

- How much do you need to sell to break even?

- How much do you need to sell to generate your expected income?

- How are you going to sell that quantity and in what timeframe are you going to sell it?

Again, it's important to be realistic here; don't set yourself up for failure by aiming for the moon in a very short period of time. That will only dampen your enthusiasm and leave you feeling extremely frustrated.

Once you have answered these questions honestly, you'll know if your business is viable and whether or not you can realistically reach your goals. As I have already said, you don't need to spend your valuable time and precious money creating a complicated business plan at this point. That isn't to say you won't need one later on, but right now you need to start selling as soon as possible; you can't afford to be wasting time on anything that is not currently necessary. Instead, put all of your research in writing and defining clear, ambitious, realistic goals. Most of all, start investing all of your time in selling your business ideas to potential clients as soon as possible.

Finally, please don't fall into the trap of finding nonsense stuff to do to avoid starting work each day. This means forgetting about perfection; you simply can't start when every little detail you wish you had attended to the day before is left undone or falls outside some self-imposed sequence of events. Rather, you have to start <u>where you are right now</u> and <u>with whatever it is that you have</u>. When you start working, remain totally focused on the actual work that makes MONEY.

REMEMBER...

Don't delay a sale because you don't have a website; don't stop because you don't have a beautiful brochure flyer; don't wait until all the ducks are lined up... shoot now to start producing your first sales. Yes, it really is that simple: prepare, SHOOT, and aim afterward, which means correct <u>after</u> you shoot your shots and not the other way around, like most everyone believes.

FIVE KEY ACTIONS FOR SUCCESS

Through my 20+ years of experience (as well as a great deal of early trial and error), I have discovered there are five basic techniques to generate business. Every time I apply them I bring in business. Period. They work for me and they can definitely work for you.

What are these five key actions for success? They are as follows:

1. Define a target audience—your potential clients— because if you can't define them, you can't find them.

Saying to yourself, "Oh, I'll do weddings, fundraising galas...and Harley biker events" is far, far too broad. You have bitten off much more than you can chew by selecting such a wildly diverse set of potential clients. It is much better to start off small with a specific client in mind than to leap into a broad, general type of activity: "Oh, I'll do grade-school birthday parties," on the other hand, sets limits within which you can work and not be overwhelmed.

2. Figure out what your client base loves and hates when you are organizing special events, particularly in light of your specific chosen business activity.

Why on earth would you propose a "Pirates of the Caribbean" theme for a general family Christmas celebration? The best way to achieve this second goal is to ask the client what they prefer instead of dictating what you believe will be best. And always be honest; if the client desires something that you cannot deliver because it is not your specialty area, have referrals ready. They will appreciate your honesty and you will have earned their respect. It could also buy you their business later on when they might have another event that falls squarely into your niche.

3. Reach your clients with an appealing message, telling them how they can get what they wish or avoid that particular thing they hate.

"What is your ideal client appreciation event?" A simple question really, but it opens the door to an open dialogue with your client. It leads them to tell you what their "shoot for the stars" event is. Once they have revealed all, ask, "And what don't you like at client appreciation events?" You have again opened the door to an honest answer. You are asking them to become an active part of creating their own dream event, and you hold the keys to the success of that event. It creates a bond that will probably end up making you many friends and gaining you many referrals if you do it right the first time around.

4. Present yourself and your services as the keys to obtaining the dream event they are longing for.

"I have been planning birthday parties for many years and I can make your child believe dreams really do come true." I don't know about you, but I want to hear how you will make my event extraordinary. By simply believing that you can, you will project that confidence in your own abilities.

5. Think BIG; become an expert. Do what you know and know what you do like no one else.

The competition is out there, you know they are. So you had better take the time to learn your craft as well as the companies you hire to create your special events. You need to know color schemes, decorating, special features that give your event that extra "oomph" to impress the heck out of your clients not once, but every time. An expert is someone who has taken the time to get to know their field like nobody else; when you do this, it will set you apart from the competition and place you way ahead of the rest of the pack. It will also earn you loyal, repeat clients–who have friends. Achieving this goal is a powerful way of literally putting money in your pocket each and every time.

IT'S ALL ABOUT YOU

You are going to learn many new things, so don't ignore what you don't already know because it could cost you opportunities. And this is also, by far, the best and quickest way to lose a sale. Your prospect asks you about a particular thing related to an event and somehow to your business, something you chose to avoid learning because you felt it wasn't for you or it was too complicated, and you respond: "Well, that's really not my specialty. I guess you should ask someone else about that."

Who was that? He or she certainly wasn't one of the people who have read my book. The importance of your business being all about you is that you can respond to any surprise with grace and tact, even if you don't know the answer right away.

The showstopper at that first meeting with a prospective client should be you. Dress properly when meeting with any potential client; this means your hair has to be "just so." your clothes clean and businesslike, your accessories polished and you must give off the air of being on top of the game—your game. At home that's not necessary, but the public, your potential clients, will notice if you appear disheveled, distracted or not very knowledgeable about your event planning area of expertise.

Do the things you do in the best possible way and don't be satisfied with anything less. Remember, "good enough" is not good enough; give your absolute best every single time you meet with a client or do an event and any work related to it. Everything you do reflects on you and your business; never forget that your client is only dealing with <u>you</u>, not a faceless, nameless employee from a big agency.

The best way to accomplish these things each and every time is to do the following:

- Be accessible at all times.

- Keep your promises.

- Respond to your mail, e-mail, and phone messages the day they arrive.

- Acknowledge your mistakes and do something to solve them.

- Always be punctual.

- Follow up when you say you will and when your client expects you to.

- Be disciplined; wake up early and at the same time every day.

- Establish a routine: exercise, take regular breaks during the day, don't go to bed late, and pamper yourself whenever you feel like you've earned it.

THE NUTS AND BOLTS OF STARTING YOUR BUSINESS

We've talked a lot about creating a plan and focusing your attention on income-generating activities right from the start, but what about the "nuts and bolts" of starting your own event planning business? These are the specific things you absolutely must, at minimum, have in place in order to successfully start up and run your business. I have put this list together based on my own experiences and lessons learned from starting my own business, so everything in here comes directly from the real world.

Some people might think there should be other things listed in this section, or that some things listed here should be taken out. However, I strongly feel these are the right things to put before you here because they are based on the knowledge and experience I've developed after 20+ years in this business.

First and foremost, starting up an event planning business requires at least some up-front budget dollars to spend on startup operating costs. You don't need a huge amount of money, but you do need enough money to, at least take care of the following items:

- Set up a workplace at home

- Open a business bank account

- Secure your domain name, hire a web-hosting ser-vice, build your website and set up an e-mail account using your domain name

- Buy your initial advertising

- Miscellaneous expenses and small needs

When you add these costs to the typical costs to start up your work space, you should expect to spend around $5,000 up front in order to get your business up and running properly on a full-time basis. You might be able to get away with spend-ing less. Of course, depending on how creative and thrifty you are this estimated amount could increase or decrease, but in the majority of cases $5,000 is a good solid baseline amount from which to begin your business operations.

Additionally, I strongly suggest you learn about these topics:

1. Creating and maintaining a website

This is not very difficult to do today because there are many excellent website building sites online such as Microsoft Office Online, among others. Once your website is up and running, you can drive traffic to it by including the URL in ev-erything you do, from business cards to advertising to e-mail messages and more.

2. Building a client list on your website

"Opt in" boxes capture the name and e-mail address of potential clients who visit your website and choose to provide you with their e-mail address. You can also set up a fast and easy auto-responder system like http://www.Aweber.com

that automatically sends out a series of messages written by you, every time you have programmed them to be sent, with valuable information related to your industry, market and services; so not only you will start building a relationship with your customers, but you'll be positioning yourself as an expert in your field.

3. Accepting credit cards

If you are not set up to accept credit cards then you are putting your business at a serious disadvantage against the competition. More and more companies both large and small are using credit cards (or purchasing cards) now as the preferred method of payment for all kinds of products and services; if you don't accept credit cards, then chances are some of your potential clients will not do business with you, period. There are a number of excellent services available that allow small businesses to take credit cards (PayPal, Google Checkout, etc.) in exchange for a small fee per transaction processed.

4. Merchant credit card accounts and how much it could cost not to accept them

Again, if you are not set up to accept credit cards, you are going to lose business right and left. The best and most traditional way of doing this is to set up a merchant account via your bank or credit union. It can be a bit more expensive to do it this way, but the advantage is that when your clients pay with a credit card, the transaction goes through your own merchant credit card account rather than through that of a payment service such as PayPal, Google Checkout, etc. Having your own merchant account is just one more way to make your business appear legitimate and substantial, which can be reassuring to clients and potential clients alike.

5. Sending large files through the web

Many e-mail providers place limits on the size of messages that can be either sent or received via their systems. This means it can be difficult to attach large documents to e-mails and expect them to get through to the recipient. If you regularly have large files to send (such as those with lots of graphics, for example) then consider using one of the online services such as http://www.YouSendIt.com to transmit these large files. It will save you and your clients the headaches that can come with e-mail inboxes being slowed down or brought to a screeching halt thanks to an oversized attachment.

6. Creating spreadsheets on Excel

You don't have to be an accountant or an economics major to use a program like Excel to create useful spreadsheets. Once you have set up the document for things like invoices, reports, and other bookkeeping requirements, it is simply a matter of inputting the most current numbers to get the most current results back. You can even set up spreadsheets to automatically pull numbers from other spreadsheets and documents, thereby dramatically reducing the manual input even further.

7. Learning to create and give PowerPoint presentations

You will likely be spending a fair amount of time working with clients as you go through the process of bringing in new business, and most often this process will involve making presentations of various types to key decision makers. It's critical, therefore, to learn how to properly use PowerPoint, because it is the most powerful presentation tool available to you. You can create presentations of all kinds, make printed handouts from the slides, use the notes sections while giving your presentation, and even include pictures, video or sound in strategic ways within the presentation.

Working from home as your own boss inevitably changes the way you spend your time, so be very careful when choosing the particular niche or specialty within the event planning industry that you are going to pursue. Once you have decided on this niche or specialty, you will find yourself spending a lot of time trying to attract clients, finding the best vendors to deliver specific services and goods for events (caterers, photographers, etc.), responding to services requests and actually running the events.

Even if you are a parent, that doesn't mean you can avoid most of the usual responsibilities that come with planning and executing a client's event. In other words, you will need to balance your life outside work with your work activities so you avoid being overwhelmed on either front. This is especially important at first when you are in the critical startup phase; you don't want anything to get in the way of giving your clients the very best possible service, but at the same time you don't want anything to get in the way of caring for your family either.

I remember that when I first started my home-based event planning business I had no sense of certainty regarding what was going to happen next. I knew I had a bunch of things to do, but most of the time I had no clue how, when, or where to start doing them. So, I started asking people more experienced than I was for their opinions, and I started reading the available sources on the subject of business management, since written materials on special event planning were nonexistent, and sometimes (actually, many times) I simply figured out for myself just how to make something work.

Somehow, with time, experience, and even a bit of luck, I learned that there was nearly always a solution to every problem I might face. There truly was no obstacle big enough to hold me back or to keep me from achieving my dream of building a successful event planning business. And once I came to this realization and started applying this approach to my efforts, all of a sudden things started to flow more naturally and I figured out how to do every task, large or small.

As a result, finding a way to "make things happen" became a matter of habit for me, and that huge "to do list" that I had at the beginning stopped making me feel overwhelmed. Instead, I just put my hands into every single thing I had to do… and did it.

So, let's take that lesson to heart right now and get moving – it's time to start doing and take action. Nothing can ever replace this single most important lesson I learned so very long ago.

There is no substitute for decisive action.

Neither meditation, nor the law of attraction, nor positive thinking alone will get your business up and running if you do not decide to take action and give your dream business the necessary form and life to become a reality.

Don't forget to join my insiders list at www.Mastering EventPlanning.com where I'll fill you in on some cutting-edge information that can help you delve deeper into this matter.

CHAPTER RECAP

1. Understand and adapt to the changes, challenges and rewards that come from running your own event planning business from home.

2. Follow the three key steps to getting your home-based business up and running:
- Set up your workspace
- Don't panic
- Reality check

3. Everything you do should be focused on the most important and vital goal of your event planning business: making money.

4. Review and apply the five key actions for success as presented in this chapter:
- Define your target audience and clients
- Figure out what your client base loves (and hates) when you are organizing special events
- Reach clients with an appealing message that tells them how you can help them get what they really want
- Present yourself and your services as the key to clients obtaining the event of their dreams
- Think BIG and become an expert; do what you know and know what you do better than anyone else

5. It's all about you. You are in charge of generating leads, finding potential clients, closing the sale and putting together a fantastic event. Remember, "good enough" is not ever good enough.

6. Pay attention to the nuts and bolts of starting your own event planning business, such as by:
- Opening a business bank account
- Securing your domain name and building your web site
- Buying your initial advertising
- Setting aside a fund to cover miscellaneous expenses and small needs

7. Take fast action to accomplish six key achievements:
- Create and maintain a user-friendly website
- Build a client list using your website
- Be able to accept credit cards
- Be able to send large files via the web
- Create and use spreadsheets
- Create and give PowerPoint presentations

CHAPTER 4

KEY BUSINESS REQUIREMENTS

"I'm a great believer in luck, and I find the harder I work the more I have of it."

Thomas Jefferson – Third President of the United States

CHOOSE YOUR BUSINESS STRUCTURE

In this chapter, I'm going to discuss some legal, accounting, insurance, and zoning considerations for your business. These are important topics because at some point you're going to have to "formalize" your business if you're serious about taking it to the level of a professional event planning operation. As distasteful and dry as this material might be, every country, town, county, city and state has its own set of rules and regulations that govern running a business. Depending on where you decide to open your business, the consequences of not complying with these governmental rules and regulations could result in fines at the least and criminal charges at the worst.

FACT:

The structure you choose for your business determines how you will pay taxes so it is critical to learn all you can about your different options and make an informed decision based on that information.

The first thing to evaluate is to choose your business structure. This is an important decision because it affects just about all of the other considerations mentioned above, but especially the issue of taxes.

From a legal perspective there are a number of business structure options, but the four major choices you have are as follows:

1. Sole proprietorship

2. General partnership

3. Incorporation

4. Limited liability company (LLC) or limited liability partnership (LLP)

We will look at each of these in more detail a bit later in this section.

Depending on the laws in your country or state, you will have certain legal options available for formalizing your business and it is important to recognize that every decision you make regarding the papers you choose to file will inevitably affect the way you keep your records and pay taxes. And this is just the beginning of the considerations you'll need to evaluate.

To reiterate what I have said in the first two chapters, this is a business, a profession, and as such you really do need to operate above-board and legally in every respect; it's the bedrock of your professional reputation.

The best recommendation I can give you is to locate and consult with a lawyer well versed in business planning and formation to get as much information as possible about the alternatives you have regarding this aspect of starting your event planning business. A good place to start is by asking friends and family who they use for legal services first, then check to see if that attorney or firm specializes in business, tax, or corporate law.

Once you have identified at least a couple of potential attorneys who can help you, it's time to make a telephone call. In many cases attorneys will not charge you for an initial consultation, so when you make that first telephone call be sure to ask about this. Some attorneys will want to take control of the conversation and do most of the talking, but don't let that happen. Remember, you are hiring an attorney to work for you so you should lay out all of your needs clearly and then see if he or she fits the requirements to meet those needs. You are the client/customer in this interaction and you should expect to be treated as such.

You'll also need to consult an accountant as part of setting up your business structure. Accountants can offer you a wide range of services, from simple consultation and guidance all the way up to more detailed services such as tax preparation, bookkeeping, auditing and other financial work.

IMPORTANT

**Although using an accountant for these regular servic-
es will be an expense to your business, in many cases
it is well worth the money purely because doing so can
dramatically simplify your life.**

So if you're "not good" with numbers, or are intimidated
by the thought of doing your own accounting and/or taxes,
or you simply want someone else with greater expertise to
handle these tasks, using an accountant may be a good
choice for you. As with finding an attorney, ask friends and
family whom they use for accounting services; you can then
work from there to identify at least two potential accountants and consult with them about your specific needs.

Both attorneys and accountants can help guide you
through the process of business formation and choosing the
best business structure for your event planning business, but
you should still have a good understanding of the four major
business structure options before making any final decisions.
Let's take a closer look at them now.

1. Sole proprietorship. This business entity is what we all
think of as a "mom and pop" operation. It is usually owned
and operated by one person as an individual or sometimes
a married couple. With this kind of structure, you will see
business names such as "Joe's Coffee" or "Fred Limerick,
Event Consulting." No "formal" business agreement is necessary because you are in business with only yourself.

The biggest advantage to a sole proprietorship is that you
have complete, 100% control of the business and you make

all of the major decisions; you hire employees or you don't; you dictate what your business will do and what it won't do; you make all of the decisions. The biggest disadvantage is that your business tax rate can be higher than with one of the other three structures, but that will vary depending on your particular circumstances and is something you need to discuss directly with your attorney and/or accountant.

Another potential disadvantage to a sole proprietorship is that you are personally liable for any litigation or lawsuits brought against your company. In other words, if a client is dissatisfied with your services and sues your business, he or she is suing you personally and your personal financial resources are potentially placed at risk. Your only protection against such liability is to take out business liability insurance, but even that has its limitations. Again, consult with your attorney and/or accountant for more detailed information.

2. General Partnership. This business entity is one you might create if you go into your event planning business in partnership with friends, family or other colleagues. Unlike a sole proprietorship, this structure requires you to draft a formal Partnership Agreement that everyone signs.

Partnerships are a bit odd from a legal perspective because, unlike corporations, each partner can be liable for the bad acts of the others even if that partner had no idea what was going on. So again, having comprehensive business liability insurance is also a crucial part of any decision to create this type of business structure. Perhaps the best thing about a general partnership, however, is that it is one of the most democratic of all business entities. Each partner has an equal say in what direction the business will take and, in the case of disagreements, a simple majority vote wins the case.

3. Incorporation.   This business entity is one we know more commonly as an "Inc." or "Corp." Microsoft, Inc. and the McDonald's Corporation are two well-known examples of this type of business structure. The incorporation process requires filing Articles of Incorporation and By-Laws with the Secretary of State in your state if you reside in the USA, but other countries have their own laws regarding formation of corporations.

In the United States, you will generally pay a relatively inexpensive filing fee that you submit with your articles and by-laws. The articles of incorporation name the incorporators and generally discuss what the company's purpose is. The by-laws establish such procedural details as meeting schedules and voting requirements to pass a resolution (action) by the board of directors.

Before you incorporate as the "ABC Corporation," it is wise to check the Secretary of State's website at the "corporate name check" section to see if the ABC Corp. already exists. You do not want to blindly incorporate without knowing whether the company name already exists because you might be infringing on someone's copyright or trademark—in which case you'll find yourself in need of an attorney for a completely different reason. Once you incorporate, you will receive a certificate of incorporation from the state.

Corporations receive very beneficial tax treatment in the United States and most other countries. This means you have a host of "tax breaks" available to you that you would not have with a General Partnership or Sole Proprietorship. Your corporate assets (work equipment, buildings, etc.) are also shielded from being attached, to a degree, if the corporation is sued and someone wins a money judgment.

But what distinguishes corporations most from the other business entities is the existence of a board of directors, or principals, in the corporation. The Board usually consists of a President or CEO (Chief Executive Officer), Vice President, Secretary, and Treasurer or CFO (Chief Financial Officer). Obviously, this means you need more than one person to create a corporation and the Board must meet regularly, record the meetings and, most importantly, maintain those records (typically the responsibility of the Secretary). The corporation's money is handled by the Treasurer. Many people mistakenly believe that a corporate structure shields individual board members from liability, but this is not true if a member of the board commits an illegal act.

It is clear that there are many more steps and require-ments to create and maintain a functioning corporation. For instance, you are required to file annual reports with the state that become public information; this means you will have to be meticulous in your recordkeeping. Finally, cor-porations can only be dissolved through a formal process.

The major considerations to keep in mind if you choose to form a corporation include:

- Who are the incorporators?

- Do you trust the incorporators?

- Who will prepare the paperwork required for incorporation?

- Are you willing to accept less control over the business because your voice only counts for a percentage of the whole Board of Directors?

- Do you have a clear understanding of all state and federal laws?

- Do you understand how to comply with corporate reporting and taxation requirements?

4. Limited Liability Company (LLC) or Limited Liability Partnership (LLP). This business entity has proven to be the most difficult of all entities due to the limits on liability of board members or partners when something goes wrong. In fact, many states in the United States have very particular rules about forming an LLC or LLP. Additionally, the tax consequences of forming a business structure of this type are different from those of the other types of business entities.

This type of business entity is widely used by attorneys and accountants because the term "Limited Liability" generally means that the partnership (read this as "the business") will not be liable for malpractice or negligence. Instead, the individual who provided the service that resulted in the negligent or bad act becomes solely responsible. In short, it protects the business from lawsuits. As with a sole proprietorship, however, you really should have excellent professional liability insurance if you choose to form this type of entity.

Speaking from my own experience, I believe the best choice is to start your business initially as a sole proprietorship. You can then choose to incorporate the business at a later date if/when you feel it's time to take that step. But please note: I am not an expert in these particular matters and I certainly don't have detailed knowledge about your own individual circumstances, so consider my general advice as just that – general advice. Before making a final decision, you absolutely must do your own homework, conduct your own research and consult with the appropriate professionals and experts to determine which business structure is actually best for your situation.

Regardless of which type of business entity you form, always remember that this is just the beginning step. In the United States, your state, city, or town likely also requires you to have a business license or some other kind of certification paperwork. This usually requires a separate application and fee and gains you the "official" piece of paper you hang in your shop to prove you are operating your business legally. You can check to see if you need a separate business license by calling your county, city, town, or state administrative authorities.

Also tied into this consideration is the issue of zoning. If you plan to operate your business from a "commercial" building there will likely be specific inspections the town or city must perform in order to approve your operation. You might need to receive what is called a "C.O." or Certificate of Occupancy that you have to display on the premises to prove you are in compliance with local codes. And, of course, there are generally fees associated with this process as well.

LEGAL CONSIDERATIONS

Other things you must know about establishing your business involve purely legal questions. It is inevitable that sooner or later you will ask questions such as:

- Can I legally do this?

- Can I claim that?

- Is it possible for me to incorporate this clause into a contract?

- Can I cancel a confirmed job and, if so, under what terms?

- What happens if they cancel on me?

I cannot stress this enough: be very, very careful when trying to find the answers to these and similar questions on your own. There are many legal websites out there that claim to be able to help you with certain documents or issues, but unless you know what you are talking about to begin with, these sites can actually get you into more trouble in the long run.

There is, quite simply, no substitute for the professional advice of an experienced and qualified attorney, as well as of an accountant.

Unlike many professions, the event planning business can be a loaded gun from a liability standpoint if you fail to take the proper measures to protect yourself legally from the get-go. The second your client signs on the dotted line, you have created a contract that is binding not only on the client to pay but also on you to deliver the event as promised in that contract. So, ask the questions in advance because if you don't, you could place your whole business in jeopardy.

One major legal issue you will confront daily if you hire people to work for you is how to treat your employee(s). You will need to deal with issues such as:

- How do you conclude an employee/employer relationship if things don't work out?

- What happens if you fire an employee?

- Can you get in trouble if you don't follow the right termination process?

Once again, I cannot emphasize enough this simple fact: You absolutely cannot ignore or avoid the things you don't already know, because if you do so then you put you (and your business) at tremendous risk. Always find out as much as possible about every legal detail of your business operations because if you don't, it can easily end up costing you exponentially more than it would have done to simply go to the extra effort of finding out the right information in the beginning.

At this point I want to give you some free advice about contracts: If you don't need them, don't create tough and protective contracts that your clients or vendors will have to sign if they want to either hire you or be hired by you. Why? Extensive contracts that include every little detail and protect you like an iron shield from everything conceivable tend to scare good clients, as well as good vendors, like nothing else.

It's much better to keep the language simple; who are the parties, what is the up-front deposit, what is the total price for the services, how will you tell each other if the contract price goes up? How will you resolve disputes? How will you proceed if the event is cancelled? You should of course have an attorney look it over, but then move forward and simply start using it. In my experience, most clients will pay you what they owe you, and if they don't you are not likely to see much, if anything, if you decide to sue them. This is the case with or without a contract filled with legalese, so you might as well keep things simple in the first place.

Remember the primary purpose of a contract; you present a contract to a client mainly to establish all of the important facts and parameters for how the job is going to be done. Through the contract you clearly establish what services you are going to deliver for an event, at what price, when, etc. The main focus, however, is to make sure that you and your client are on the same page on all the major issues.

Please, if at all possible, avoid using a contract with lots of language mentioning all of the costly consequences and penalties your client might incur if he does not follow and comply to the very letter with every clause of the contract, or how much he might have to pay in terms of legal fees if you sue him.

I will reiterate, try to obtain a professional contract that is specially tailored to sell your event-related services. Pay a lawyer to create one or to proof yours, or download one of the many legal documents online and adapt it to your own needs – it's a heck of a lot better than doing it yourself, especially if you don't know anything about legal issues.

ACCOUNTING AND TAXES

The topic of accounting and taxes is really quite simple: hire an accountant, keep excellent records and invoices, and pay your taxes on time.

That's it.

Nothing is more stressful, annoying, time and energy-consuming and costly than not having decent and well-organized account records. If you do not keep good records and/or pay your taxes on time, sooner rather than later you will have the tax authorities – state and federal – breathing down your neck and investigating your business operations.

So, do your homework and find yourself a good accountant that you can afford. And by this I don't mean a basic, tax preparation service; I mean a professional accountant who understands your business and who can help you do your numbers and make better business decisions. In fact, I would go so far as to say you literally cannot afford **NOT** to have a high quality, professional accountant working on your behalf.

KEY TO SUCCESS

When you have the right professionals performing these kinds of critical tasks for you, you have made the kind of decision that can mean the difference between succeeding and failing.

Yes, it will cost you some money to retain the services of a good accountant, but the money you invest in this area will pay huge dividends in both the short term and the long term. When you invest the money necessary to ensure your accounting is clean, straight and accurate, you are really investing in the infrastructure necessary to have a successful, long lasting, and profitable event planning business. This may sound extreme, but it is the truth.

As you go about the process of choosing and working with your business accountant, here are a few "nuts and bolts" items to keep in mind:

- Learn how your accountant plans to calculate and pay your taxes; ask why he or she intends to use that approach and why it is preferable to other options available

- Find out exactly which expenses you are allowed to deduct and which ones you cannot, and be very clear on the details of how you must document those items correctly

- Set up a schedule of regular contact and communication with your accountant; this ensures you are both current on what is happening in the business and up to date on the potential tax and accounting implications

- Find out how your accountant stays up to date with tax regulations, and how he or she plans to evaluate changes as they come along in terms of their effect on your event planning business

By making the effort up front to choose a good accountant and maintain a solid working relationship with that accountant, you are greatly increasing the potential for the success and profitability of your event planning business.

ZONING

Zoning is an issue that comes up with every home-based business, and is an area where it is easy to get confused or run into problems. As a general rule, starting a home-based event planning business is not going to run into zoning issues in most places **IF** you do not have customers, vendors or suppliers coming to and from your business location on a regular basis.

In other words, as long as you run the business using your computer and your own living space and do not use that space in a commercial manner, you are generally going to be okay. However, most event planning businesses quickly outgrow this narrow set of limitations and so face the issue of determining local zoning requirements and coming up with the best way to stay within them.

For instance, let's say you go into the specialty area of being a theme party organizer; chances are, you're going to end up with props and other items that need to be stored, vendors and/or suppliers delivering supplies to, or picking supplies up from, your home or any number of other logistical concerns. It's easy to see how zoning can quickly become an issue.

To determine the zoning requirements for your location, you'll need to check with one or more local authorities to determine the rules by which you'll have to abide. Some examples of authorities to contact include:

- Your city, county, or town zoning administrator

- Your homeowner's association (if applicable)

- Your apartment manager (if applicable)

Remember, failure to abide by zoning requirements may seem trivial but it can actually trigger some fairly hefty county, city or town penalties ranging from monetary fees to immediately having to halt business operations until zoning issues are resolved. So, save yourself a huge amount of potential hassle and lost business by checking on zoning issues up front so you can be sure you're meeting all requirements from the start.

BUSINESS INSURANCE

One of the most overlooked but absolutely critical things to have in place right from the start is business insurance. You might not think of this as a critical item because let's face it, it's just another expense you have to pay at a time when money is probably really tight. But just as you wouldn't own your home without having homeowner's insurance or own your car without having car insurance, neither should you own your event planning business without proper business insurance.

Business insurance comes in a variety of types and forms but, according to the U.S. Small Business Administration, the most common categories are the following:

- **General Liability** – Covers general risks and claims related to negligence, damage (bodily or property), resulting medical expenses, legal costs related to lawsuits, settlement bonds or other judgments necessary if you must go through an appeal of a lawsuit.

- **Product Liability** – Covers general risks and claims related to the manufacture, distribution, and wholesale sale or retail sale of products and services rendered by a small business. It also applies to legal claims related to negligence, warranty, product defects, insufficient warnings, or directions.

- **Home-Based Business** – Covers potential losses and issues that are unique to the needs of a home-based business, such as business property losses, business data losses, disability, professional liability, injury due to advertising or promotional activity, and crime and/or theft of business property or assets.

- **Worker's Compensation** – This is required in every state if you have employees who are directly employed by the business itself. The amount and type of coverage will vary depending on the state in which you operate your business, so if you have direct employees you'll need to check with your state for exact details. However, in most cases, worker's compensation insurance is not required for several categories of workers, including you as the business owner, contractors, vendors, and independent suppliers.

SUGGESTION:

I strongly encourage you to get at least two or three quotes comparing coverage and costs, because there can be significant variations in these things from company to company.

- **Business Interruption** – Covers losses to a business caused by unexpected interruptions caused by events such as fire, natural disaster or other types of catastrophes generally beyond your control. Policies vary in terms of the types of interruptions covered and the duration of those interruptions.

It is well worth your time and effort to consult with an experienced insurance professional to get a better idea of the exact types and combination of coverage that's best suited to your particular needs.

The areas you will particularly need to pay attention to include:

- Replacement and/or repair of business assets such as props and any other equipment in the event of theft or damage

- Protection for your business in case employees, vendors or suppliers cause damage to a client's property or other event venue; most cities and/or towns will require you to have proof of this kind of insurance in hand well in advance of any event you plan and execute

- Coverage for claims of negligence, including damages, legal defense, legal awards, and appeals.

Again, I strongly recommend you consult with an experienced insurance professional about all aspects of determining the right combination of business insurance coverage and actually obtaining that coverage for your event planning business. This is not an area in which you should attempt to skimp or save money by choosing "bare bones" coverage, because the risks to your business are just too large to ignore.

LOCAL PERMITS

Nearly every kind of event you will plan and execute will require some form of local permit. In some cases, the venue you're using will already have general use permits in place (hotels, event facilities, etc.), but you will almost certainly be required to obtain special permits for using other venues such as parks, community centers, and city or county property. Other reasons why you might need a special permit include elements of an event such as lighting fireworks or having a band play outdoors or after certain hours. Or, let's say you're organizing a festival for your community in a park; in that case, you'll definitely need some form of permit (or even multiple permits, in some cases) from the local authorities.

Other examples of situations in which you'll likely need a permit include:

- Conducting a raffle to give away a large prize, such as a brand new car

- Playing pre-recorded music; may require a permit due to a local musicians union

- Using animals as part of a party (i.e. pony rides at a kid's birthday party, exotic birds at a jungle-themed party, etc.)

- Offering valet parking

- Cooking food on-site rather than pre-cooking it off-site

- Serving alcoholic beverages

- Carnival rides or activities

You might be surprised at just how many situations will call for some form of a special permit so it's not a bad idea to develop a good working relationship with your local authorities; this will make it easier to go to them for information in advance and make them more likely to work with you cooperatively throughout the permitting process.

Remember, these kinds of details might seem boring, but they are very necessary in the world of professional event planning. Paying attention to these and the many other details along the way forms the very bedrock of your success and expertise in the event planning industry.

It's all about knowing the rules and operating your business within those rules; if you do so then you'll be much better able to build a successful, profitable, and long-lasting event planning business. If, however, you choose to ignore the rules or simply fail to educate yourself on what they are then you will not succeed. Period. It really is as simple as that.

USEFUL LINKS AND RESOURCES

Here are a number of useful links and resources for you to access regarding information and issues we've discussed in this chapter:

- **Business Taxes:** www.irs.gov Click on the section marked "Businesses." There you will find answers to many common questions as well as good advice on what is and is not permissible when dealing with federal business taxes.

- **Legal forms:** www.legalzoom.com This and similar sites generally charge a fee for each form you access, so double check to be sure the one you select is appropriate for your city, county, state or country, and is written in the correct language (English, Spanish, etc.).

- **Accountants/Attorneys/Small Business Advice:** www.sba.gov and www.score.org. The first link is to the U.S. Small Business Administration, perhaps the best and most comprehensive resource of all for small businesses in the United States. The second link is for an excellent non-profit organization where retired business owners and executives offer advice and guidance to small business owners. It is one of the best resources of its kind and I highly recommend it.

Please note that these are all resources specific to the United States; if you live in a different country, then you will need to identify the appropriate resources to use to accomplish your objectives.

If you haven't done so yet, join my insiders list right now to stay up to date on this and other important event planning topics – You can join for free at www.MasteringEventPlanning. com.

CHAPTER RECAP

1. Research and understand the various business structures and choose the one that's right for your business and its needs:
- Sole proprietorship
- General partnership
- Incorporation

- Limited liability company (LLC) or limited liability partnership (LLP)

2. Research and understand the variety of legal issues you might encounter during the operation of your business, such as:
- Contracts, clauses, cancellations and claims
- Employer/employee relationships
- Vendor/supplier relationships

3. Research and understand the issues related to accounting and taxes. Hire a high quality business accountant and then set up a regular schedule of consulting with and working with that person. Be prepared to spend some money for these high quality services; it will save you money, hassles, and potential legal problems in the long run.

4. Research and understand all zoning issues related to your home-based business. This includes checking with your city, county, or town administrator, your homeowner's association, your apartment manager, and any other authorities as set up in your state or country of operation.

5. Obtain high quality business insurance, consulting with an expert to determine the right kinds and amounts of coverage necessary to fully protect your business and your property. Examples of common types of insurance include:

- General liability
- Product liability
- Home-based business
- Worker's compensation
- Business interruption

6. Identify and comply with all local permit requirements. Check with the venue to determine if they already have permits in place and consult with local permit authorities to determine if there are additional permits you need to obtain for each particular event.

CHAPTER 5

CATEGORIES OF EVENT PLANNING SERVICES

"There is only one social responsibility of business — to use its resources and engage in activities designed to increase its profits without deception or fraud."

-- Milton Friedman, American economist

One question you will no doubt ask yourself over and over again is, "What kind of event planning professional do I want to be?" You see, in the event planning industry we continually find new services and new technologies being integrated into the range of services we provide; however, there are some categories of services that are most common and regularly used to plan and manage most types of events.

In this section, I'm going to talk about these most common categories of products and services so you can begin to decide where your interests may lie for your unique event planning business. Most of these categories fall into one of three main areas of event planning professionals: the event planning generalist, the event planning specialist, or the event services supplier.

GENERALIST OR SPECIALIST?

The first and most important question to ask and answer is this: Are you going to be an event planning generalist (essentially a logistics planner coordinating many different types of events) or an event planning specialist (essentially a service supplier with planning capabilities, specialized in some types of events only)?

Now, since the primary purpose of this book is to provide you with the necessary tools and advice to start your own successful home-based event planning business, I feel obligated to give you my best advice on answering this question. And that advice is this:

I believe that becoming
an event planning specialist is the best way to go.

Working as a generalist or a specialist may, at first glance, seem to be very similar because both of these require you to organize many types of events, coordinating as many suppliers as needed along the way without having to invest in any special equipment yourself (at least, not in the beginning).

However, working as an event planning generalist will mean you will be responsible for planning many different types of events and, based on my own expertise and 20+ years of experience, you will very likely struggle to get things done properly and efficiently if you take this approach. Trying to meet the huge variety of needs and solve the myriad problems inherent in these types of events is just too big and too complex to handle well, especially at the beginning of your event planning career.

On the other hand, working as an event planning specialist allows you to focus your energy, actions and efforts on that certain type of event that interests you the most. For example, you might become a wedding planner, a party planner for family events, a theme event planner for corporations, a party planner for children under 8-years-old or the like. The list of possibilities is nearly endless. I suggest you become an expert in one or two fields of your choice, and expand the reach of your services when you feel ready to move to the next level.

REMEMBER...

Another advantage of becoming an event planning specialist is that, based on your expertise, the chances are high that people will call you first when they need an event like the one in which you are an expert.

Here's an analogy to consider: You need an original, specialty towel to coordinate with the décor in your newly remodeled bathroom, so you set out to shop for this particular towel. There are two stores to choose from in your neighborhood: "All Towels Mega Store" and a generalized department store. Which store are you going to shop at to find your original, specialty towel?

Chances are you're going to shop at the "All Towels Mega Store" because it is a specialty towel store that is more likely to have exactly what you are looking for. The generalized department store, on the other hand, carries a broad array of items across a broad array of categories so finding that specialty towel there is far less likely.

The same principle applies to the event planning business. If you become a specialist in the event planning business, chances are you are going to stand out from your competition and that will translate into much better sales for you.

In my case, the specialty for which I am most recognized is themed event design, planning and production for corporations. Focusing on this specialty has been the secret and the key to my success. Of course, I do plan many other types of events other than just theme events or parties, and you will too; this is true no matter what specialty you decide to undertake. However, because of my specialized experience and expertise, my clients tend to think of me as the first choice option when they want to throw the ultimate themed event or party for their corporate guests.

Regardless of whether you choose to be an event planning generalist or specialist, planning even a single event will usually involve liaising with a number of suppliers of different goods and services and then coordinating their activities. Your role is to add value for the client wherever possible, such as by negotiating the best possible prices and contract terms from each vendor and then passing those savings on directly to your client. The way you make your money is to earn a commission from each supplier or add an incremental cost margin to your charges (also called an agency fee), and all the while your client benefits by the job being done on time, within budget and under the most advantageous contracting conditions, but I will talk about this particular topic in the following section.

Within the category of event planning specialist there are even more possibilities for offering even more specialized services by becoming a supplier of event service specialties. In the next few sections, we'll look at some of these specialties and the issues surrounding this approach in more detail.

EVENT SERVICES SUPPLIER

Professional event planners deal with a wide range of vendors and suppliers, including what are known as event services suppliers. If there is a particular area where you have a special talent, expertise or simply a passion then you might consider becoming a supplier for that kind of event service. You can still offer event planning services, but you would be more of an event service supplier, specializing in your own service, with planning capabilities, rather than a full scale event planner, either a generalist or a specialist. An example of this would be if you decided to be an event caterer, but you also coordinated additional services for your client such as providing a band, the valet parking, the videographer, the florist and other services related to your particular core business.

FACT:

Regardless of the specialty service you decide to offer, be sure to do your homework and find out the exact steps necessary to start your business off on the right foot.

If you decide to enter the event planning industry as a service supplier, it is very likely that you will need to make an extra investment in special equipment for the particular activity you decide to feature. This can be a significant obstacle when you're just starting out and working from your home, as it can create challenges related to space, storage, and zoning constraints, among others. In most cases you'll probably need to look very seriously at starting your business in a commercial space rather than from your home.

So what kinds of event service supplier might you become? The list is long and varied, but the most common supplier services that professional event planners deal with include the following:

- Catering, including servers and other catering staff

- Floral arrangement

- Tents, stages and dance floors

- Audiovisual equipment for presentations

- Lighting

- Photographer

- Videographer

- Ice sculptures

- Wedding cakes

- Sound equipment

- Dee-Jay

- Bands and musicians

- Models and hostesses

- Talent agency

- Party favors

- Bathroom trailers

- MCs and animators

- Special effects/pyrotechnics

- Linens

- Rentals

- Furniture

- Themed décor

- Live entertainers

- Staffing

- Security

- Registry control

- Costumes

- Decorative fabrics

- Language interpreters

- Valet Parking

- Graphic design

- Printing

- Games and inflatables

FACT:

Depending on the event service you choose to offer, you'll need to plan for continuing investments in even more equipment and/or technology in order to stay current in that area and offer your clients an assortment of the latest trends.

One of the most powerful arguments for starting out as a special event planner rather than as an event service supplier is the lower amount of money you will need to invest up front. Setting yourself up in business as a special event planner is almost always a great deal less expensive than setting yourself up in business as an event service supplier, which will most likely require you to make a much larger initial investment.

If you are interested in becoming an event services supplier from the start, I recommend you develop a good working relationship with an established business in your field of interest. Why? Because this will give you an opportunity to learn a great deal very quickly through critical hands-on experience; truly, you have no idea of just how much you can learn and just how much time, money and energy this can save you.

You will quickly gain a good idea of which aspects of that particular service or activity you like (or do not like) and if you discover that that area of the event industry isn't really right for you then you can simply stop doing it without having invested a great deal of money into it. This allows you to move on and find something else that truly motivates and excites you.

Another option is to start selling the particular event service yourself but actually fulfill client needs by contracting with another service supplier who is already in business and familiar with that particular activity. This gives you the advantage of being able to work with clients right away, while avoiding the prospect of investing heavily in tools or equipment right up front.

You'll instead be working with someone who "knows the ropes" of that service area and have the opportunity to learn from them and their operations. Please note that if you choose to take this approach, then you absolutely must have a formal legal contract with that third-party provider to cover your bases.

But what if your business idea for becoming an event services supplier involves a very new or unique piece of equipment or technology? Your options in this situation include pursuing a loan to acquire what you need, or starting with something you can afford in the beginning and then moving on to the next level and buying that particular item you have in mind when you have enough cash flow to do so.

Regardless of whether you decide to become an event planning generalist, an event planning specialist or an event service supplier, if you want to be successful you absolutely must make the effort and spend the money it takes to become the very best in your field. Now of course nobody expects you to be the "very best" right from day one; that simply would not be a realistic goal. However, you do need to focus all of your energy, time, and efforts on improving your skills and abilities each and every day. Remember, competition in the business world (no matter what business you enter) is more vigorous than ever before; if you don't make the effort necessary to truly excel in what you decide to offer the public, then chances are your new business endeavor is not going to go very far.

PRICING YOUR SERVICES

It is crucial that I say this up front: If you don't understand how to charge correctly for your products or services it will be very damaging to your business.   In fact, it is a major reason why many businesses of all kinds do not succeed in making a profit; they simply do not know the right way to go about setting their prices at a point which maximizes sales while also maintaining a satisfactory level of profit.

Another major reason why businesses (and especially event planning businesses) end up failing is that they are not aggressive enough about maintaining an acceptable level of profit margin for their services.   It's critical then that you always make sure you are getting a fair (and well deserved) profit for your work.

IMPORTANT

Never spend too much on an event in an effort to impress a client. You run the risk of spending every cent the client has paid with nothing left over for your profit.

But in the event planning business, figuring out and charging the "right" price for both your business needs and your client needs is not as simple as you may think.

Let's face it: Asking people for money is hard. When I started my event planning business, I was very hesitant when it came to charging what I thought was the "right" price; I was worried it was too high and that my services would be so expensive that I'd never win as many clients as I needed to succeed.

What I had to learn though, is that as with any service, what constitutes the "right" price depends on several factors such as:

- The marketplace

- The cost of goods used

- The cost of services or overhead to deliver the event as promised

- The value your services represent to the client

- The complexity of any particular service

- The amount your client is willing to pay

Because the event planning business is largely based on the client's emotions, I didn't want them to think that I was trying to rip them off if they were ever to discover my costs in terms of vendors and suppliers and from that amount figure out just how much profit I was making from their event. I believed or, more accurately, I was conditioned to believe, that prices should be charged in strict relation to the man hours invested in doing a particular job. This might work in some industries, but it most definitely does not work in the event planning industry.

It didn't take me long to discover that prices for products and/or services in the event planning industry should actually be charged based primarily on the results and/or benefits received by the client. In other words, the "right" price includes the value of your unique services in addition to the cost of specific vendor services or products used in a particular event.

So leaving behind the "man hours = reasonable price" mentality is crucial to your success.

THE BOTTOM LINE

You are delivering them something of tremendous value, and your product or service is worth every single cent of the client's investment.

Whether you decide to be an event planning generalist, a specialist, or an event services provider, you still have to make sure your clients are happier with the results they obtain by hiring you rather than by hiring your competition. This, in turn, translates into opportunities for developing relationships with long-term clients who will prefer to hire you again, even if it means they have to pay a little more by doing so.

It's okay to charge more for your services than do your competitors, but if you do so then you absolutely have to make sure the extra cost is well worth it to your clients. You must always "over-deliver," every single time, exceeding your client's expectations and leaving them completely satisfied with your work. Delivering what the client wants plus a little extra-special something is much better than trying to be "fair."

And don't think you're being greedy by charging a little bit more either. If you don't charge a little extra and earn the value you deserve for your services, then you'll soon find yourself barely breaking even or, more likely, losing money overall because your prices are not set at the right level. Charging a cheap price (called "low-balling") for the sake of undercutting your competition will not help build your business and will, in fact, damage your business, especially when you are starting from scratch.

So, how should you go about determining the right price to charge a particular client for the services they will receive from you? Here are a few ideas to help you with this process:

- Research how much the leading providers of the product or service you intend to provide are charging in your area

- Research how much your clients are already paying for the same or similar event services

- Check with your local Chamber of Commerce or Small Business Administration Office for information about local costs; these organizations will usually have fairly current statistics on the average cost of certain services in your area

But remember, as you're setting up your pricing, you've got to strike a balance between charging prices that are low enough to attract clients to your relatively new business and being a better quality (but higher priced) alternative for your clients in the long run. It's critical to start your business with the sole desire and exclusive goal of being the very best at what you do. It is only with this kind of mindset that your business will be profitable and hopefully quite lucrative as well.

It's easy to fall into the trap of charging low prices to start with, merely because you're a new market player. While this might attract clients to your new business, however, it also creates the expectation in their minds that your prices are lower. Once this expectation is established, it becomes very, very hard to raise your fees later on, because your clients already see you as a low-price provider.

One of the worst mistakes I made when I was starting and growing my business was charging low prices in order to gain more clients in the beginning and then feeling that I was doing a job essentially for free because my prices were so very low. It was an important lesson and one that I will never forget; that's why I'm passing it along to you here.

Another drawback to charging low prices—and believe me I've seen this happen many times—is that it makes clients suspicious. They will start asking themselves, "Why is this so inexpensive? Why is it so cheap?" This, in turn, leads them to conclude that the low cost must be due to lack of quality, lack of professionalism, and perhaps even desperation for their business. Obviously, none of these are good things.

KEY TO SUCCESS

Don't waste your time, energy, and opportunities; charge the right price (even if it is a bit higher) from the beginning and your business will prosper in the long run.

So never, ever charge a client on the cheap side just to gain a contract for that one event. If you do this then you run the very real risk of losing that same client the next time around when you try to raise your prices and charge more in line with the "real" value of your services.

Finally, don't base your prices on the salary you earned at your former job. Remember, owning a business will cost you money up front in the short term because you must incur expenses you didn't have while you were working for someone else as their employee. As a result, your prices as an entrepreneur should most definitely not be set on the same basis as if you were an employee of another event planning business or of any other business. You must calculate everything to cover the event costs, your fixed expenses and your profit –which must be significantly higher than your former salary–, otherwise, why would you be willing to start your own business if you were to make the same money than when you were an employee?

PRICING METHODS AND OTHER WAYS TO MAKE MONEY IN YOUR BUSINESS

There are a number of different methods for determining what prices to charge for your event planning services. Whether you are a general event planner, specialty event planner or event services supplier, here are the most common approaches used to determine appropriate prices and charges:

- By the project

- By fixed price

- By flat fee

- Based on commission

- Using discounts

- Using mark-ups of other services

- By the hour

Let's take a look at each of these in turn.

By the project

This is my preferred method for pricing out my services because over the years I have discovered it works the best in most situations.

The first step in this pricing method is to calculate your fixed costs and your variable costs. Fixed costs are those prices that do not change no matter how many people attend the event. Examples of fixed costs (also called overheads) include the following:

- Venue rentals

- Entertainment/DJ/speaker fees

Variable costs, on the other hand, are those prices that change depending on how many people will attend the event, how many services your client requires, and how expensive (or inexpensive) those services are in regards to the level of quality your budget allows you to provide. Examples of variable costs include the following:

- "Per plate" meal costs

- "Per place" setting special floral arrangements

Once you have calculated your fixed costs and variable costs, the final step in determining the price you'll charge the client is to add in your associated profit margin. Profit margin is typically set at some specific percentage above the total costs (fixed + variable); this amount is sometimes also referred to as the "mark-up" charged to a client.

To accurately determine the appropriate profit margin necessary to generate an overall profit for your business, you'll need to do a "break even" analysis. In other words, you need to figure out how much you would need to charge in order to merely break even on the costs. Breaking even, of course, means you don't make any profit on the event; you stand to gain the experience, of course, but experience doesn't pay the bills at the end of the month. The crucial element in this calculation is variable costs; you have to figure out the highest possible amount they could be.

So, let's say you are planning an event where the variable costs change based on the number of people who attend; you need to figure out the minimum and maximum number of people who are likely to attend in order to figure out the range of what your variable costs might be.

When you're setting your prices, it's critical to include not only the fixed and variable costs of the project, but also to place an appropriate value on your own time and expertise. You want this amount to be representative of the value you provide; if it is not high enough

then you essentially end up under pricing and giving away your work.

It should look something like this (please note, these are not real prices; they are simply examples used to illustrate this general idea):

For 100 guests
Meal cost $10 per plate = $1,000
Room cost = $100
DJ cost = $100
Stage cost = $100
Auditorium cost = $100
(Total costs (variable + fixed) = $1,400)
Profit margin of 25% = $300
Total project price = $1700

Here is another example of an event services provider. Let's say you are an event videographer and sell edited videos of events that include the highlights and most important aspects from an event.

The value you place on your skills should be determined based on researching what other similar videographers are charging, as well as what the marketplace will bear for the level of service and quality you provide. And of course the overall project cost would also take into account hard overhead costs such as your investment in the camera and other equipment, cost of supplies necessary for recording and editing, electricity and air conditioning for your home editing studio, and gas, insurance, and time spent obtaining the necessary supplies.

So let's say, just as an example, that you will spend $50 on recording materials and, after factoring in the investment in your professional equipment, software and all the items listed in the previous paragraph like gas and air conditioning, you end up with a total cost of $100 in order to make a video for a client. With this in mind you decide to charge the client $200 to shoot the event and provide a five-minute edited version of the video.

This seems like a great price, doesn't it? Well, here's the bad news: it only seems that way and the actual price is not appropriate for what you're providing to the client. Why? Because it fails to take into account everything else that actually put you in business in the first place, such as the expense of creating and maintaining a website, the cost of a business telephone line, the business stationery and, most importantly, your expertise and the time you invest in recording and editing the video.

FACT:

Your labor is not free; it is an important part of the overall project cost.

Remember, when figuring out what to charge for your own work there are two distinct parts to this amount: labor and expertise. Most people treat these as one and the same, when in actuality they are two completely different concepts. Most people fail to accurately capture the value of their expertise, but even worse, they also fail to accurately capture the value of their labor.

Think of it this way; you would never work for someone else if they failed to pay you for your labor, so why would you fail to pay yourself for your labor in your own business? If you can avoid just this single very damaging mistake and always accurately calculate your business costs, then you will find it much easier to maintain your bottom line profit. If you fail to make this calculation accurately, however, you will have difficulty maintaining your bottom line profits and may very well end up not enjoying doing what you once loved.

The bottom line here is to charge a decent, fair, and competitive rate for your services and never work for free.

By Fixed Price (for additions)

When you charge by the project it sometimes happens that there are additional costs or services that were not initially foreseen by both parties in the original deal. In this case you will need to deal with these additional costs or services, usually by adding a fixed price or surcharge for the additional item(s).

The key to being able to do this is to always include in your project contracts a clause or section (signed by the client) that stipulates there will be additional charges in this kind of situation. I have found that many people balk at the term "surcharge" because it has lots of negative connotations (for instance, have you seen the many different surcharges charged by the airline industry these days?) so I prefer to use the term "additional costs," "fixed price additions," or something similar.

So, when might you need to add a surcharge or a fixed price addition? A common example is when you are planning a banquet event where more guests actually attend than originally planned. This happens all the time, actually; someone decides to bring along an extra friend, or more family members show up than you originally thought would make it. In order to accommodate this kind of change, you can either add a small fee onto the per plate cost or generate a revised per plate cost for the entire project to cover the added cost to you of providing the extra meals.

So, working with the example from above, you figured the overall event cost to be $1,400 if a maximum of 100 guests attend. This translates to a per person cost of $14; but what if actual attendance is 120 people? Well, it obviously increases the cost of the meals by $200 and the amount of your overall profit margin by $40, so you need to account for this extra cost plus the appropriate profit margin somehow. You might add a surcharge of $240 on the entire event, or execute a contract addendum for the fixed rate of $240; this is really your call to handle as you like. If you are not sure what to do, find out how other service providers in your region deal with these situations so you can stay within the boundaries of what is accepted in your particular community.

By Flat Fee

Several lawyer friends of mine charge their clients a flat fee for their professional services, reasoning that clients want to know in advance exactly how much they will spend for legal services. This is not an unusual desire, especially when you consider that hourly rates for attorneys can be as high as $400-$500 per hour, and the client really has no control over how many hours the attorney is going to spend on their particular needs.

It is much more attractive to the client for the attorney to quote the flat fee cost, which then puts the responsibility on the attorney to complete the project within that dollar amount if he or she plans to make a profit. For the attorney, however, this kind of arrangement works best if the client agrees to this flat fee amount on an ongoing basis; the reasoning is that some months the actual time spent on that client's needs will be less and some months it will be more, but overall the amount of services provided will fall within the value of the flat fee charged.

As an event planning professional, you can take a flat fee approach also and, just as with the legal profession, you too should only agree to this kind of arrangement if the client commits to using your services on an ongoing, predetermined basis, such as for a 12-month period or for a minimum amount of money to be invested in an event. With this kind of agreement, it is typical for the flat fee to be established based on a percentage of the total amount of services you will have to coordinate for the client.

For example, you might charge a 20% flat fee for every dollar spent by the client on any particular event. This means they pay $1.20 on the dollar, so, while your costs might be $100 for an event, the client will actually pay you $120 for that event. Be careful though not to confuse this flat fee approach with the commissions that your suppliers pay you, which is a completely different thing.

Based on commission

As an event planner, you will generally receive a commission from suppliers and/or vendors each time you hire them for an event you're coordinating; you might also make commissions for referring them to other clients who end up making a purchase. You can make money off supplier/vendor commissions as long as you hire them when producing an event, or if you recommend a vendor who is actually capable of doing a good job for your client and he subsequently pays you a commission.

This level of pricing applies when working with a supplier as part of your team, and also when you do nothing more than make a referral. It is critical, however, that the supplier and/or vendor you work with or recommend be someone reliable whom you truly trust. Why? Because many times that supplier and/or vendor will be doing the job without any supervision from you and at the same time collecting money directly from the client. If that supplier and/or vendor does not perform at an acceptable level, then it reflects badly on you and can damage your client relationships in the future.

Remember that in most cases the commission passes to you <u>after</u> the job is completed, so you should not make this type of referral if you are not 100% certain of the quality of that supplier/vendor, their reputation for keeping their word and their record of complying with the obligation to pay you the agreed upon commission.

As you should have figured out by now, event planning is a reputation-based business heavy with client emotions. If you work directly with or send someone to a shady operator, you will do damage to your own business and name in both a direct and indirect manner.

Using Discounts

Unlike a commission, using discounts is a reduction in the price a service supplier charges you.

For example, let's say the price for the catering service for a particular event is $5,000 but the caterer offers you a 10% discount for bringing repeat contracts to their business. If you charge your client the regular price for this part of the event and do not pass along the 10% discount, then you end up making more money on that particular event.

The difference between commissions and using discount pricing is that the commission means the supplier collects the total amount of the sale price and, subsequently, pays you some percentage of that price you both agreed upon. In the case of a discount, however, the supplier reduces their price by an agreed-upon percentage and charges you this reduced price. The discounted amount never changes hands and thus you are able to make money by charging your client a mark-up which is equal to or a little higher than the original price of your supplier. In this way you can make a profit without overcharging for the service, while also reducing the risk of not being selected by that client because you charged a price that was far more expensive than the average market price for that particular service.

Some event planners take the approach that they offer their clients the benefit of doing the entire job of coordinating an event and getting the best possible deals for the client, period. In these situations they do not charge the client more than the actual price charged by each supplier and they do not inflate the overall budget of the event.

In other words, they offer their services for free to the client and focus on making their money from commissions and/or discounts they get from suppliers. Quite frankly, this is an extremely difficult way of building a profitable business and paying your bills. It isn't hard to imagine a situation where you could either devote your time to a very low budget event that requires the same amount of work, or even more, from you than a regular budget event; so, which would you prefer to do? You could easily end up working for nothing, or close to nothing, and we already talked about that— don't ever work for free.

I suggest you instead consider commissions as extra rather than as your primary stream of revenue, and that you gain additional sources of income such as by charging a mark-up or an agency flat fee besides the discounts and commissions.

Using mark-ups of other services

Either you get a commission or a discount from your suppliers or you don't. But regardless of your arrangements in this area, you can also charge a mark-up to your clients depending on the basis on which you are doing business with them. So for instance, if you have already informed the client that your only charge is the agency fee, then you wouldn't want to charge a mark-up on other services.

It is generally not a good idea to charge your clients an agency fee and a mark-up; charge either one or the other, not both. Or, for example, if you promise your client to do the job with the idea that you will only make money on commissions negotiated with the suppliers and promising them to get the very best deals, then, once again, you simply can't mark up those services if you want to have a return client. If you are charging your client an agency fee and he finds out that you are also making money by marking up the services you are coordinating, he is going to consider that dishonest conduct and will not wish to do business with you anymore.

It's crucial that you are as clear as possible with your clients regarding these matters. If you want to charge by the project, that's fine. If you want to sell based on the argument that you are getting the best deals for the client and making money out of commissions you negotiate with suppliers without affecting or inflating the price, that's also fine. But never, ever, say you'll do one thing and end up doing another. Believe me, in this business, there are many ways to earn income. Your job is to make certain that none of them conflict with each other or with your client's best interests.

By the hour

Event planning is not usually billed out by the hour, even though some jobs could potentially be priced this way. I strongly advise you to avoid this pricing method as much as possible, because it is extremely difficult to accurately estimate the number of hours you will dedicate to a project. What's more, the client is going to check and scrutinize the final bill all the more when you use this method and will often compare your hourly charge to his or her own hourly fee.

This works to your disadvantage because in most cases your fee is going to be considerably higher than the amount earned by your client in his/her job when we are talking about corporate events and you are dealing directly with an executive who works for that company (which, of course, it will be, because why on earth would you open a business in the first place, when you could be making more without having the hassles and risks of that business?) and this client is going to automatically assume you are charging prices that are simply too high. When this happens, your fees don't appear justified and you put future business with that client at serious risk. There are, however, situations in which you can charge some services by the hour, like a live music band, or charge a fixed price for extra hours at a venue, when an event extends its duration.

Finally, never agree to provide your services for free in exchange for the promise of future contracts. This is a common scam used by clients who simply want to get something for free and never intend to use your services again. If a potential client wants to see your work first and then decide whether to give you a paid contract in the future, you should simply tell that client your method of operation is to charge full price for the first contract and then consider offering a discounted price on the next one.

BUDGETING

Regardless of the pricing method you select, be sure to consider every possible expense in your project budget. Be as specific and as clear as possible about the budget when discussing prices with your client, and whenever possible show the client a comprehensive spreadsheet to clearly show how you arrived at your budget numbers.

The last thing you want to be is an event planner who arrives at the site of the event only to be confronted with hidden costs or forgotten aspects of pricing that you were not considering from the very beginning during the budgeting phase. These are the kinds of last-minute surprises that neither you nor your client will want to pay for, which is really bad for your business, bad for your finances, and perhaps worst of all, bad for your reputation as a professional event planner.

Why is this so important? Because every possible detail that could be missing is something that can also cost money and therefore impact your profit margin. If no other party to the event is covering a particular detail (such as a power generator when it's needed or the rigging of equipment, etc.) then include it in your budget.

Budgeting skills are also crucial because you are working both for and with your client. If you don't know how much that person is prepared to spend for whatever event you are planning, then it doesn't really matter what your prices are. Remember, your job is to create an event working within the means of your clients as well as your own.

So, if a family can only afford $10,000 for a wedding, why would you budget their wedding event to cost $25,000? What's more, since you are just starting out and interested in building up your reputation and business, why not strive to make that $10,000 super special and memorable, even if it means you make a little less profit than you originally hoped for? The value will increase for you because of the repeat business and coveted referrals that a super-satisfied client will send in your direction.

This is where your communication skills are absolutely cru-cial to a successful business arrangement. The more clearly you communicate with a client about what he or she can and cannot do within their dollar limits, the better off you will be. And of course, this also opens the door for you to sug-gest alternatives that might cost them less but still earn you a decent profit. As a result, excellent budgeting skills will win you more clients in the end, while poor budgeting skills or even ignoring the realities of budget limitations will do major damage to your business.

There is one more common situation I want to warn you about; sometimes you will come across a client who is interested in organizing some type of event and intends, let's say, to charge a fee at the entrance and/or for the food and beverages served to attendees at the event. This person might just try to convince you to accept a percentage of the money made in this way at the event as your service fee rather than agreeing to a service fee up front.

Never, ever accept this type of agreement.

Why not? Let's say you are an event professional and own sound and lighting equipment, and somehow a person suggests the two of you should do business together. He offers to organize a concert at a local venue with one renowned rock band from the community and agrees to take care of every task involved. He asks you to provide all of the sound equipment and lighting for the concert at no cost. He tells you the concert will be a huge success and that you two will split the profits 50-50 after covering all expenses. These profits will come from sources such as money collected for tickets at the entrance, sales of food and beverages inside the venue, and other potential income. He promises you will make a small fortune and it doesn't look too hard to do this project.

Sounds like a good business deal, right? Wrong.

REMEMBER....

If you have the budget and the clear intent to organize an event to promote your business and get it noticed, then you must do exactly that.

In my experience, this type of deal never goes well, even though to a novice event planner it might seem like a good business opportunity to gain publicity and get noticed. The sad truth is that kind of arrangement will almost certainly result in a loss of money and wasted energy, and worse, it is unlikely anyone is going to take notice of your contribution to the event and decide to hire you for a future event.

Put all of your focus into promoting your business in the best possible way, but always remain aware that to accomplish this will cost you work and money. Once you focus on this, then your investment can yield the results you seek and you can reach the goal of promoting your business and getting noticed by your target audience.

Regarding this topic, I still have a few tricks-of-the-trade up my sleve. If you'd like me to share them with you, join my insiders list right now (it's free) at www.MasteringEventPlanning.com.

CHAPTER RECAP

1. Based on my experience in the event planning industry, I strongly recommend you pursue a career as an event planning generalist only if you are truly organized, focused, and have high command to lead people into accomplishing ambitious projects completely different from one another.

2. Becoming a specialist allows you to focus your energy, actions, and efforts in a particular area that interests you. Additionally, you develop the kind of knowledge and expertise that makes you the "first choice" of clients looking for that particular type of event or activity. Your business will

stand out from the competition and generate more sales and more profit.

3. Another potential focus for your business is to become an event services supplier. This area of focus generally requires a greater financial investment up front and on an ongoing basis in order to obtain any special equipment or materials necessary to fulfill your specialty services.

4. While I recommend starting out as an event planning specialist, if you want to focus on being an event services supplier, it is a good idea to establish a good working relationship with an established business in your field of interest. This allows you to learn from someone else and develop critical hands-on experience.

5. It is vital to understand how to correctly charge for your products and services. Failure to establish appropriate pricing is one of the major reasons why businesses fail to make a profit and eventually fail overall as a business. Figuring out the "right price" to charge involves considering a number of factors, such as:
- The marketplace
- The cost of goods, services, and overheads
- The value your services represent to the client
- The complexity involved in providing a service
- The amount the client is willing to pay

6. Don't be afraid to ask for money in exchange for your services. What you do has value and you deserve to be compensated for the expertise and results you provide. It's okay to charge more than the competition if the services you deliver are of exceptionally high quality and are worth the premium price you charge for them. It helps when setting prices to do some extra research such as:

- Determining what other providers are charging in your area
- Determining what clients are already paying for the same or similar services
- Determining the right balance between low enough prices to attract clients and high enough prices to properly value your services and make an acceptable amount of profit

7. Common pricing methods include the following:
- By the project
- By fixed price
- By flat fee
- Based on commission
- Using discounts
- Using mark-ups of other services
- By the hour

My preferred method of pricing is by the project, because it allows you the most flexibility and is well suited for the majority of situations.

8. Excellent budgeting skills are necessary to ensure proper pricing and profit margins. Always consider every possible expense in your project budget; leave nothing to chance and don't assume another vendor or supplier is going to cover an expense unless it is specified in the contract. Use a spreadsheet program to create detailed and comprehensive budgets; this allows you to be specific with your clients and demonstrate clearly to them how you arrive at your budget numbers.

CHAPTER 6

MARKETING, ADVERTISING, AND PROMOTION

"The aim of marketing is to know and understand the customer so well the product or service fits him and sells itself."

- Peter Drucker, Management Thinker and Writer

DEVELOP YOUR BUSINESS IMAGE

Your public image communicates everything about you and your business, and is in fact your business image. Obviously, this means when you are designing your business image, it's important to take into consideration every visual aspect of your business that potential clients will see, including yourself.

So, if you decide to organize bachelor parties, for instance, make sure your image doesn't contradict that purpose. In other words, you would hardly help arrange an evening for "the boys" dressed in a either a tuxedo or a pair of Bermuda shorts with no shirt. Instead, you would probably choose a professional, but slightly-casual suit for approaching potential customers and the managers of the establishments that will host the food, beverages, and entertainment.

You absolutely must think about the way you dress, your logo, your colors, the way you address your written communications, your website, your brochures, and other pieces that make up your overall company image. Everything people see, hear, read, and experience about you and your business has to "mesh" together seamlessly so when you meet with clients for the first time, your image translates into a direct and immediate connection with you as the owner of a professional business operation and with the quality services you provide.

DEVELOP YOUR UNIQUE SELLING PROPOSITION

KEY TO SUCCESS

Becoming a successful event planner means that, just like Domino's Pizza, you must create your own personal "brand," a unique selling proposition that sets you apart from the competition.

What do you think of when I mention Domino's Pizza? Few if any people would associate this business with anything other than fast delivery of pizza. Their original, unique selling proposition, the thing that set them apart from all others, was their promise of delivering your pizza within 30 minutes or less, or the pizza was free. It was catchy, it was attractive to customers, and no matter how much others tried to imitate it there was no escaping the fact that this unique selling proposition belonged to Domino's Pizza alone. And even today, although they no longer offer the 30 minute guarantee, the overwhelming perspective people have of Domino's Pizza is that they are a popular and successful pizza delivery business.

It is critical from the very beginning to establish your brand and maintain brand consistency by using a selling point unique enough that people will associate it with your particular event planning operation. Your unique selling proposition expresses clearly and succinctly that which makes you different from others who do what you do. It is what makes you different from all the rest of the marketplace and is a powerful way to make your customers identify you and your business.

Remember, people are looking for a variety of experiences and memorable visions that only professional event planners can turn into reality, so your unique selling proposition needs to position you as a provider of such memorable experiences. You must be seen as a problem solver and a coordinator of flawless events; the "go-to" person to rely on and ensure things are done properly so the host will not have to worry; the person whose services impress and pamper guests; and the one to seek out and find the latest and most creative alternatives and ideas in the industry.

In my own business, the unique selling proposition is "Sell your Ideas... We can Build Them." With this USP, we clearly communicate to customers that when it comes to creating any idea whatsoever for their special events, we are the ones to go to. Why? For a number of reasons, of course, but primarily because we have a one of a kind production facility; we're capable of making practically anything for a special event; we can produce nearly every imaginable kind of decoration, prop or stage, as well as many other things; we have a wide variety of talent and entertainment alternatives; and if there's something we can't do ourselves, we have a huge array of event services suppliers at hand to recreate and complete any themed event concept.

What's more, you can be the event planning business with the best deals with suppliers, the provider to whom the client pays a fair price but gets more; the one who finds a flexible way to adapt to the client's needs by offering more alternatives to choose from, and so much more. In all seriousness, this list can be practically never-ending.

Find your USP.

It's really not that hard; just take a look at what problems or situations your customers want to solve first of all, then offer them that and turn that offer into a USP.

To properly develop a USP you must be crystal clear regarding your event planning focus. For example, let's say you love prom parties and you want to plan high school proms. You would not then advertise for corporate special events in the same advertisement or in the same manner as you would a high school prom organizer. That does not mean you cannot do both, but since the bulk of your income will come from a particular type of event (in this case, high school proms) this is the event you promote the hardest and into which you invest the most money initially.

If you do this, then when school administrators look in the local business directory for prom planners, they'll find you listed; additionally, your corporate letterhead will reflect that proms are your specialty, as well as reflecting what it is that makes you different from other professionals also doing high school proms. The same will be true of your business cards, your presentation materials, your website and everything else associated with your business. You might also use a tag line such as "Creative Prom Party Concepts to remember forever," which is then featured prominently in your advertisement in newspapers, on the Internet and in the telephone book.

DEVELOP YOUR SALES PITCH

What is a sales pitch? There are a number of different ways to define "sales pitch," but the one I like to use most is the following:

A sales pitch is a communication tool or message used to present information about your business that is designed to inform the listener, initiate consideration of using your services, and set the stage for closing the sale.

The sales pitch then, serves multiple purposes in a variety of situations and is not something that you can just throw together on a whim or with very little thought or consideration. Each part of your sales pitch, each word and each phrase, must serve a purpose and work together to present the essence of your business efficiently, effectively, and creatively.

To develop your own sales pitch, take some time to think about and answer the following questions:

- What is the brand or image you are selling?

- What are the key features of the products and services you offer?

- What are the key benefits of the products and services you offer?

- Why should the listener or potential customer choose your products and services?

Now take your answers and think of them in terms of the audience you are trying to reach. Using the previous example of focusing on planning high school proms, think about your target audience of school administrators. What are the answers they need to hear in order to understand the value you offer and be willing to pursue your services? Put yourself in their shoes and take into account the issues they face when it comes to planning their school's prom, issues that might include things like:

- Limited budget

- Legal requirements for a school-sponsored event

- Limited time to put toward planning activities

- The need to include a student committee in the planning process

- The ability to enter into a contract that meets with the school district's procurement and contracting procedures

These are the things you need to touch on in your sales pitch, but remember you don't necessarily want to go through this complete list every single time you present it. What you need to do is prepare three versions as follows:

- **Full length** – Three minutes long at the most, to be used during telephone conversations and other pre-arranged contact with potential clients. The purpose is to provide enough detail about your business to get the potential client interested and start a more in-depth conversation about their needs.

- **Half length** – One minute long at the most; to be used during shorter conversations, such as cold calls to prospective clients, or answering emails or online inquiries from potential clients. The purpose is to provide enough information about your business and your business brand to entice the potential customer to be interested in hearing the full-length version.

- **30 second length** – Sometimes also called your "elevator pitch" because it should be no longer than the time it takes to ride with someone in an elevator, which is typically about 30 seconds. The purpose is to give the potential customer a glimpse into your business, communicate your business brand, and present yourself in a manner that is consistent with your branding and promotional activities.

IMPORTANT

Practice all three of your sales pitches out loud; do them in front of a mirror, enlist the help of friends or business acquaintances to role play with you, and video tape yourself as well.

Start by preparing the full-length sales pitch and then condense it from there to create the half length and then the 30-second length sales pitches. Write it down initially, but then practice saying it out loud; you're going to find that what sounds good aloud is often quite different from what reads well on paper. In this case, you want to focus entirely on the verbal, practicing your pitch out loud until you have it memorized and sounding professional.

Your goal here is to practice, practice, and practice some more until your sales pitches flow smoothly, sound polished, and present your business (and yourself) in the very best manner possible.

NAME YOUR BUSINESS

Naming your business involves a variety of issues to consider, some of which are creative and some of which are legal. As I mentioned in Chapter 5, my specialty is corporate theme events, so I named my business "Sarao" which is a Spanish word not used very much today meaning "elegant dancing party." Most people don't know right away what "Sarao" means, so they ask me; this question gives me the opportunity to explain the word and deliver my "elevator pitch," so helping them to both learn the word and generate interest in my business.

They tend to remember my business then, because of the unique name, its significance to what I actually do and the elevator pitch I share with them which, although short, effectively communicates the key attributes of my business. It emphasizes how we can re-create any concept for a theme event in a unique, spectacular, and enjoyable fashion. I tell them that Sarao means fiesta, and that we take our name seriously when it comes to guaranteeing a once in a lifetime and memorable experience to all attendees to one of our *Saraos*.

Then guess what? When the time comes that they want to organize a memorable and fun themed party, I am the one who quickly comes to mind to help them do the job. The bottom line for creating what I will call an "effective" business name is to make it creative enough so that it, and you, will stand out in a crowd. This is especially true if you live in a larger city where there are many people serving as event planners in your chosen field of expertise.

This means you have to be very, very creative. A name like "Texas Event Planners" probably isn't enough to attract a lot of interest, but a name like "Magical Event Productions" on the other hand, stirs up imagination and creates an expectation that somehow your events are different from those of the competition.

From a legal perspective, as discussed in Chapter 4 you will need to make sure your business name is not already registered to someone else in the state or country where you set up your business structure. You might also consider consulting an attorney regarding trademarks if your business name also includes a unique design or logo as will be discussed below.

The bottom line though, is that the key to a good business name is that it indelibly links you and your business to the service you deliver in a manner that is uniquely different from the competition.

CREATE YOUR BUSINESS LOGO

I urge you to put some time and effort into creating a nice logo that doesn't look outdated. You always want the logo to tell the potential client something about your business; it might be one of your personal initials, the first letter of the business name, or an image related to some aspect of your specialty focus. Choose a color scheme that is eye-catching yet appropriate to portray and communicate the image you want to convey. So for example, if your focus is on planning environmentally friendly "green" events then you don't want your logo to feature a purple unicorn or a bright red racing car.

Do some research into current trends of logo design by visiting one of the many websites specializing in logo design. Look at their portfolios of logos and pay attention to the ones that you find most attractive and memorable. Many of these websites offer logo templates you can purchase, making it easy to pick the one that best matches your business image and right away have access to a professional logo for use on all of your promotional materials.

If you are willing to spend a little more money, then consider hiring a graphic designer to create a custom logo for you. While this decision is entirely up to you, I urge you to consider just how vitally important your logo is to your business and how you communicate about your business. Should you trust something this important to chance or to someone who is a novice in this field? Probably not. Remember, if you do not know how to do something right the first time, hire someone to do it for you so you do not expend extra money correcting a mistake that didn't have to happen in the first place.

Legal issues also come into play with your logo because it can also serve as your trademark. You will need an attorney to file the appropriate trademark registration papers for you and to make sure you reserve that mark for your business alone. That way, if anyone uses it, you will have legal recourse to make them stop.

There is nothing nicer for a business to have than that special "pop" in a publication courtesy of a stand-out logo. In practical terms, this means you want to also make sure your logo translates well into both color and black-and-white. Some publications you use might only offer black-and-white, or color may be prohibitively expensive, so having both options is a good idea. At the end of the day, we all want to succeed and having a great logo only moves you closer to success.

Exerting a mediocre effort for a so-so logo might get you a few clients, but if you really want to stand out in the crowd, then do whatever it takes to create a logo that's unique, memorable, and especially suited to your event planning business.

CREATE YOUR PRINTED MATERIALS

Printed materials represent your business to whoever views them, so shouldn't they be an accurate representation of your brand? Remember, these are the things that "speak" for your business when you are not there to speak for it personally, so it's worth the time and energy to make sure they are exactly right for this purpose.

At minimum, you should invest in the following printed materials:

- Letterhead stationery

- Business cards

- Regular letter-size envelopes

- Big envelopes to hold a lot of papers such as manila envelopes or even larger self-sealing "mailer"-type envelopes; these can be paper or some sort of plastic, depending on their size

- Presentation folders with interior pockets

- Blank note cards with your logo

Even though many of your written materials will be delivered digitally (emails, attachments, etc.), many of these materials will also be delivered in person in the form of a physical proposal. Hard-copy presentations will always create a better impression on your potential client if they are printed on branded materials (those items that bear your distinct logo, business name and contact information).

CAUTION

Be careful that your branded materials are not overly expensive looking or too fancy; in my experience, using materials that are too expensive looking can actually hinder your chance of winning a project because they leave the client wondering if your prices are too high or if you will be unable to stay within their budget requirements.

I also like to recommend investing in a few "leave be-hind" items that are customized with your logo and business information. These are things like pens, pencils, Post-It notes, or other office items. You don't want to buy the most expensive of these things, but neither do you want to buy the cheapest either. Focus on choosing items that the potential client is highly likely to actually use from day to day and keep handy on their desk. This keeps your business logo "front and center" every time they look at the item, plus if you choose items that are useful it also subtly communicates to the client that you are focused on identifying and meeting their needs.

Never go to a presentation empty-handed; this means that even if you are making your presentation electronically, always bring along a hard copy to leave behind with each person attending the presentation. This gives them something concrete to take with them after you leave and serves as a reminder, not only of the services you can provide, but also your business brand and feel.

A common mistake I'm seeing more and more often relates to business cards. There are lots and lots of software programs and pre-designed business card templates available that allow you to design and print your own cards using your own computer. As inexpensive and convenient as these are I strongly recommend you <u>do not</u> make your own business cards. This screams to the potential client that you do not have much money and, even worse, they make you come across as being cheap. They tell the potential client you don't believe it's worth it to make a little investment in a decent business card and leave them with the impression that you don't plan to be around for long.

I know this sounds harsh but, in this business, image is everything. And showing the client how much effort you put into something as small as a business card speaks volumes to the impression you leave them with by the end of your presentation.

I cannot emphasize enough the importance of making sure that everything, printed or not, makes you look good and not bad; and also that it's consistent with your personal and business images. Event planning, again, is a serious, professional occupation. The materials you present must convey this if you want to create and maintain credibility wherever you do business.

BUILD YOUR EVENT PICTURE PORTFOLIO

Every time you do a job for a client, right from day one, start taking pictures of your events. You have no idea how much this one little activity that seems so trivial helps me sell my services to other clients down the road. Instead of trying to describe to a potential client how I'm planning to set up table decorations, for example, I can open up my portfolio of pictures and literally show them exactly what I have in mind. In case you don't have any photos, bring any visual materials like renders, layouts, or other graphics that can help you picture your ideas and event concepts in a clearer manner, and again, start taking photos of your events as soon as you can.

To do this well however, you need to invest in a good quality digital camera. Thankfully these can be had for as little as $200 to $300 and are available with lots of features and in a compact, convenient size. This makes it easy to always have your camera in hand, ready to photograph every aspect of your work from the set-up to the tear down. Be very creative with this by taking photos from different angles, using the close-up and panoramic view settings and playing with light and shadow. You also want to take photos of the venue all "dressed up" right before the guests arrive; after they arrive, make sure you take plenty of photos portraying people having a great time at one of your events.

FACT:

Smiling faces and happy people convey a good message that they are enjoying themselves because you planned a wonderful, magical event.

Having good photos for your portfolio is valuable because it shows potential clients what their events could look like. It also allows them to see that people like your work.

Remember, we live in a visual age of communication. People are attracted to beautiful images and you can expect to sell many jobs by presenting a wonderful photo album put into, say, a power point presentation to highlight what makes your business unique. It is true that a picture does in fact speak a thousand words. Make it work for you.

TRADITIONAL ADVERTISING TOOLS

There are three main venues for advertising outside the Internet which you can use to attract potential clients: print, direct mail and magazines/other media. All three of these cost money and can become quite expensive quite rapidly, so you have to be very careful and focused in how you use these traditional advertising tools. I don't suggest that you do a lot of advertising in these formats in the early stages of your business, but you do need to at least be familiar with them and understand when it's useful to take advantage of the promotional value they offer.

Print advertising refers mostly to newspapers and other local publications. The cost of this kind of advertising depends on the size of the ad, the number of times you want it to appear or "run" in the publication and the style (including color) of your advertisement. What's more, it's nearly impossible to truly measure the effectiveness of this kind of advertisement.

Direct mail is not cheap either; you have to pay to print the mail piece, pay to obtain the mailing list of addresses, pay someone to process the mailing and deliver it to the post office, and of course, pay for the postage itself. Even worse, the vast majority of direct mail advertising goes directly into the trash can. Professional marketers are pleased if they get a response from 1% to 2% of the people who receive their pieces; this means 98% to 99% of the pieces are wasted and do not generate any kind of response. As a small business owner with a limited budget, this is almost certainly not the most effective way to spend your advertising dollars.

Magazines and other media are also generally priced very high, but they do offer you some opportunities to focus your advertising in places where you know you're going to reach your target audience. However, unless you are investing in an ad in a proven advertising vehicle which clients always pay to appear in (like a special events magazine) and that you know actually works well, don't waste your money.

CREATE A WEBSITE

For your event planning business, a good quality website could be one of the most, if not the most important and effective ways to market and promote your business. It's like having a salesperson working for you 24/7, showing potential clients all about your business and communicating the key messages you want them to receive.

There are many ways to start a website depending on how computer literate you are; some people understand computer languages and the basics of website design, while others don't want anything to do with the actual process of designing their own website and prefer to hire someone else to create it for them. Or, you might be someone who wants to give creating your own website a try, falling somewhere in between these two extremes of experience and preferring to use one of the many "do it yourself" programs and templates available. The truth is that today, literally anyone can create a website.

Don't let yourself be overwhelmed regardless of how you decide to go about it. The easy availability and vast reach of the Internet is so great that you might also tend to psych yourself out of doing the basics. "But where do I begin?" you may well ask yourself. Hey, I've been there, and that's what I am here to help you with.

Start by understanding that most people try to find information on the Internet by doing a basic search. Most people "Google" something to learn more about it, right? And to "Google" something you have to enter words that match what you are trying to find. In computer-speak these are called "keywords." For your business to be found online, it requires the website to use certain words that trigger the search engines to locate your business... and probably several thousand others as well.

The most obvious keyword for your business type will be "events"; "event planning"; or more specifically, "party planners in Texas"; or even more specific still, "theme party planners in El Paso Texas." If the words "party," "planner," "El Paso" and "Texas" appear in your ad or in your site, the likelihood is higher that your website will appear on that search list.

Search engines also allow you to pay money to "optimize" the probability your site will pop up when these keywords are put into a search field, and today many website creation sites allow you to make search engine optimization part of a "package" website deal. So obviously, keywords are important when creating a website, and the more specific these words are to your particular event planning business, the better.

Next, you should create a domain for your website. Think of a domain as your cyberspace address. Using the example above, Google's domain name is www.google.com. Government domains in the United States are easily identifiable by the ending .gov; for example, see www.irs.gov, the website for the federal Internal Revenue Service. Most nonprofit corporations in the U.S. have domain names ending in .org, while businesses such as yours will more likely than not reside in the .com universe. (Example: www.yournamebusiness.com)

Once you have named your business, you can have a domain based on that name, but be careful not to make the domain name so complicated that potential clients forget it, confuse it with something else, or don't bother to try to figure out how to spell it. Once you actually purchase that domain name, nobody else can use it once it is registered through any number of sites like www.godaddy.com. But it isn't enough to come up with a domain name; you also have to find a company to host your website.

MSN Office Online has a free website service that is as simple to use as the Windows program and which requires little to no knowledge of html or xml coding (the chains of characters that create an image or text on a website). After one year, you must pay to continue to use the site, but among all other similar sites I think it is really one of the best if you are a beginner.

You need to host your site, and good hosting service is provided by www.hostgator.com. Here you can tailor your website creation to your actual computer skills. They offer everything from advanced website creation using your own software to a point and click version similar to MSN Office Online. The fees are somewhat higher than other sites, but their service is amazing. To learn more about the many hundreds of website hosting sites companies just Google "website hosting" and start scanning through the ones that attract you.

By the time you think about keywords and register a domain, you probably have a good idea of what you want your website to look like. The designing aspect is the fun part and allows your creativity to shine through to potential clients who discover your site online. You can always find someone else who specializes in website design to create your site for you. This is the quickest and most efficient way to get a site up and running quickly, but it will cost money (sometimes a lot of money). Whether you want to make that investment or not is up to you.

You can also purchase software programs such as Adobe Dreamweaver that allow you to create a website at home and upload it to your hosting site (each hosting site has instructions on how to do this). I would generally advise against buying web design software unless you are extremely computer literate, because oftentimes the coding necessary is quite complicated and requires a great deal of practice to master. I suggest instead that you use the templates available via your hosting site to get things up and running quickly and easily. Most of these designs are professional-looking, easy to use, and allow you to change colors and add your own photos.

REMEMBER...

No matter how you go about creating your website, you want to make sure it reflects the image you truly want to convey.

Make your website informative, both about your services and other topics of interest related to your activity, and educate your potential client by providing quality content. Make sure you have a way to capture every visitor's name (it is usually called a "guestbook") and e-mail addresses so you can start building a follow-up database list of potential clients.

With this database, you can deliver all sorts of informative and promotional materials, such as articles, tips for creating memorable events or the latest trends and ideas related to your area of expertise. Be careful though, to send only practical information that they can benefit from, or else you will be branded as a spammer and your e-mails will be deleted.

Your website should also include a generous selection of high-quality images of your events. Remember, people form opinions within seconds based on what they see and not necessarily what they read; even certain colors have different impacts. Dynamic websites heavily feature the colors red or blue, while greens are reserved for more peaceful sites. Believe it or not, there is a whole psychology built around website color and photographic content to enhance the ability to advertise various goods and services. Before you leap into the realm of the Internet feet first then, it pays to do a little research, establish your comfort level and then get started.

NEW MEDIA ADVERTISING TOOLS

There is a whole range of new media advertising tools available for marketing and promoting your event planning business, most of which can be very effective as well as cost-efficient too.

For instance, email marketing is an extremely effective tool in the event planning business. Use your database list referred to in the previous section and look into using client contact lists from other businesses in your industry in exchange for, say, an endorsement or mutual link on your website.

You would be wise to look into autoresponders too. As I mentioned before, an autoresponder automatically sends out a series of messages written by you, every time you have programmed them to be sent, with valuable information related to your industry, market and services, along the way generating client database lists you can use to e-mail your promotional materials to potential prospects. There are many very good software programs to choose from, such as www.aweber.com, and a number of other full featured websites offering various types of autoresponders for sale. And while it's true many people delete e-mails, you are much better able to target your messages to your specific audience at a cost that is nominal; you literally have nothing to lose by using this powerful tool.

There are general Internet advertising options as well, which I believe are more efficient and more effective than the traditional advertising tools discussed previously. As with anything new, however, you will not know how to effectively advertise online overnight; it is a learning process. A good place to start is by learning the basics of how to use the powerful tool known as Google AdWords.

Take a look at the website www.adwords.google.com. The concept is simple; when people type in keywords related to your event planning business, your ad will pop up in a banner along the right side of the web page that displays the search results.

This tool is effective because you already know the person searching is looking for an event planner, so your ad is targeted to the right audience. And if they see your ad and decide to click on it they go directly to your website and very well could become your next paying client. The beauty of this system too is that you only have to pay for ads when someone actually clicks on them; this fee is truly nominal in light of how much business this feature can generate.

The latest and greatest trend in new media advertising tools is social media. This is a broad category of communication tools and avenues that includes blogging, RSS feeds, forums, discussion groups, etc., along with the very well-known social media websites like Google+, Facebook, LinkedIn, and Twitter. The popularity of these tools has exploded in the last years, and businesses of all kinds are finding they absolutely must have a presence in this arena if they want to compete, let alone succeed.

TIP:

Once you have established a presence for your event planning business on these websites, start finding ways to use them creatively as promotional tools.

A number of excellent tutorials and guides on how to effectively use tools like Google+, Facebook, Twitter, and LinkedIn are available, but the best place to start is on these websites themselves. Take the time to go through their online "how to" information, paying special attention to their Frequently Asked Questions and Getting Started sections.

You can learn a lot just by paying attention to what others are doing even if they are not in your industry. For instance, look up the Pepsi page on Facebook, the MTV page on Google+, and the Twitter page belonging to MSNBC. Notice how these very different companies all use these tools to reach out to their target audience with proactive information, offering useful resources, opportunities for interactive communication, and creating a sense of "belonging" among their followers.

Blogging is another effective way of reaching your clients and potential clients. Why? Because a blog is a quick, easy and convenient way to regularly put out information that will be of interest to your clients but in a format that's casual, interesting and personalized. You can plan your blogs out in advance to a certain extent, so they correspond with your overall marketing focus.

For instance, let's say you're prospecting for Christmas party clients in June or July. Why not put together a couple of blog entries about your favorite Christmas party event ideas? This allows you to reach out to your blog readers with a topic of interest but in a way that's friendly, conversational, and easy to read. What's more, it plants the idea in the reader's mind that it's time to start thinking about the Christmas party, making them more likely to either call you themselves or be interested in talking with you when you make that prospecting call.

These are all ways you can use social media to promote and market your event planning business as well.

EFFECTIVE PUBLIC RELATIONS FOR YOUR BUSINESS

The activity known as public relations refers to how you promote your business and services in a special way within your particular community. I have listed a number of ways to get your business noticed, some of which have proven more successful than others for me. But just because something has not worked as well for me does not mean it will not work well for you because every event planning business is unique. It is important to evaluate your options, try different things and find the activities that work best for your unique needs.

- **Media Appearances** – Submit press releases to local media outlets and follow up with them to arrange media appearances to discuss some interesting aspect of your business. Most media organizations are constantly on the lookout for unique and interesting content to cover, so if you give it to them then they will cover it and provide you with some "free" publicity.

- **Expert Commentary** – Establish yourself as an expert in the event planning field or in some unique aspect of your particular area of business focus. You can do this by writing articles, contacting local media outlets, and working with the local Chamber of Commerce or the like. When you create opportunities to speak to others, with the description "expert" in front of your name, it gives you instant credibility and is bound to attract business in your direction.

- **Socializing** – Never underestimate the value of simple, old-fashioned socializing. Whenever you are at a party or other social event, always try to speak a little about your business (remember the elevator pitch we talked about?) and be prepared to hand out maybe a business card if a person is really interested and asks for your card. Never, however, hand out your cards as if you were passing out treats to children on Halloween night. Remember, it is after all a social event and if you want to get invited back again sometime, you need to use your best professional discretion.

- **Networking** – This method of getting new clients is highly effective and strongly recommended. So, what is networking anyway? Bluntly put, it's selling your business to total strangers through people you already know or do business with. For instance, let's say you have a baker who works for you on an event. You two become friendly and have a good working relationship, so when the event is over you say, "Hey, Serge, thanks for your great work. Do you know anyone else who might want this kind of event sometime?" And watch what happens. You've made Serge feel good about his business as well as about you, and so he will be willing to recommend you to his friends and colleagues (a) because he knows you will bring him in on it too, and (b) because you're one heck of a nice person and ultra-professional, and he had a good time working the event for you. So don't hesitate, get out there, network as much as possible and you'll be pleasantly surprised at the results you generate.

- **Association Memberships** – These memberships are good for networking and learning about the industry, but they can be expensive and provide little in the way of measurable return. Unless there is a very specific, targeted association that will allow you to network and truly advance your business, I recommend you look elsewhere for more effective public relations options.

- **Convention and Visitor Center** – This might seem a little farfetched at first glance, but in fact getting in touch with your local convention and visitor center is an excellent idea. There, you can place a supply of your brochures that are made available to a variety of people, such as people coming into your city or town to attend an event. Also, people attend conventions sponsored by corporations which – you guessed it – hire event planners to create the event at that very same convention center. Make sure you get to know the key contact people at these venues and maintain a good relationship since they can recommend you when people inquire about event planning services, especially if you are in the convention and conference market.

This particular topic is mission-critical to always planning the best events. Stay up to date with the latest information by joining my insiders list at www.MasteringEventPlanning.com.

CHAPTER RECAP

1. Develop your business image. This is critical because it communicates everything about you and your business.

2. Develop your unique selling proposition (USP). This is critical because it sets you apart from the competition and associates specific skills, specialties, and abilities with your business. Identifying and communicating your USP requires complete clarity regarding your event planning focus, the value you offer to your clients and the reason(s) why they should choose your event planning business for their needs.

3. Develop your sales pitch; it is a critical communication tool for presenting information about your business in a way that informs the potential customer, initiates consideration of using your services, and sets the stage for closing the sale. Your sales pitch should answer questions such as:

- What is the brand or image you are selling?
- What are the key features and benefits of the products and services you offer?
- Why should the potential customer choose your products and services?

4. Prepare three versions of your sales pitch, practicing them out loud until smooth:
- Full length – Three minutes or less
- Half length – One minute or less
- 30 second length/Elevator pitch – No more than 30 seconds long

5. Choose a name for your business that captures the essence of your services, your personality and your professional focus. Be creative and select a name that links your business to the services you deliver in a way that sets you apart from the competition.

6. Create a business logo that's attractive, interesting, creative, and distinctive. Don't settle for something outdated or boring, because that conveys the wrong message about your business. It is well worth spending a bit of money to access a database of logo templates, or even better, hiring a graphic designer to create a custom logo. Pay attention to the color scheme as well, thinking in terms of how the logo will reproduce in black-and-white as well as in full color.

7. Create printed materials to represent your business, keeping in mind that these materials will speak for your business when you're not there to speak for it yourself. At minimum, you need the following:
- Letterhead stationery
- Business cards
- Letter size envelopes

- Large envelopes
- Presentation folders with interior pockets
- Blank note cards with logo

8. Take pictures of every single event, from start to finish, to build up an event picture portfolio. It may seem trivial, but taking pictures to put into a portfolio is one of the single best things you can do because it allows you to literally show potential clients what you are capable of doing for them.

9. Use traditional advertising tools (print advertising, direct mail, magazines) sparingly but in a focused manner.

10. Build and maintain a high quality, user-friendly website where you can show your work, collect customer contact information and communicate specific messages and information about your business. Optimize your website for search engine rankings, testing various keywords and phrases to see which of those related to your business are most-searched.

11. Tap into the power of new media advertising tools because they are extremely effective and extremely low cost. Use tools such as:
- Facebook
- Twitter
- Google+
- Blogging
- RSS feeds
- Forums
- Discussion groups
- Email updates
- Electronic newsletters

12. Use effective public relations techniques and tools such as:

- Media appearances
- Expert commentary
- Socializing
- Networking
- Association memberships
- Convention and visitor center contacts

CHAPTER 7

CREATE A STRONG TEAM

"The way a team plays as a whole determines its success. You may have the greatest bunch of individual stars in the world, but if they don't play together, the club won't be worth a dime."

- Babe Ruth, Major league baseball player

THE IMPORTANCE OF CREATING YOUR TEAM

Although you are just starting out in the event planning industry and likely have a limited amount of money available to you, it is unwise to go at it entirely alone. You will have more than enough work to do just selling your services and running the events, let alone taking care of the day-to-day issues such as making sure bills are paid on time and service providers are contacted as necessary.

There are plenty of tasks that need to be done, and I strongly recommend you consider hiring at least one professional to help you with these activities. It does not have to be a direct employee; an independent contractor will do nicely, provided you choose the right person. And while delegating duties is difficult for most business owners at first, you really do need to create a good team of people to help you be successful. These are the assistants, suppliers, helpers, and vendors who will help you deliver memorable events on time and within the set budget, as well as to manage the many tasks necessary to build your business.

REMEMBER...

The Internet is a great tool for finding suppliers; it is probably the quickest and easiest way to find people because their websites allow you to check their portfolios.

CHOOSE YOUR SUPPLIERS

When you find someone who you think might be a good "fit" with your business and/or event, you can put them to the test by asking for more information and see how they respond. You will be able to judge for yourself whether they respond quickly enough, whether they make an effort to understand your particular needs, and whether they charge a competitive price, among other things. You in effect become the job interviewer, so pay attention to all of the responsibilities that come along with that role.

As the interviewer, you should feel perfectly comfortable asking for references and verifying any information the supplier offers. This is called doing "due diligence," making sure they are who they say they are. Failing to do due diligence can not only cost you money, but if the supplier has a bad reputation in your community it can damage your reputation as well.

Remember, it is your reputation and business license on the line, so it benefits you to know as much as you can about a potential supplier before you commit to use the services of that particular person or business. Pre-screening will save you potential broken contracts and other legal conflicts that could arise from failing to do your due diligence.

Another good approach is to call one or more local hotels and ask for a recommendation on whatever event service you are interested in contracting out. Identify yourself clearly and be truthful about your needs, then simply ask whether they might be able to help you find a local supplier. The best department to handle your inquiry would be the one handling conferences, conventions, special events or even banquets. This is a very effective technique I used when I started my business, well before Internet searches were available.

Contact other event planning professionals in your area to ask for referrals to service suppliers, and also talk with your family and friends as well. Chances are they have been involved in some type of event, whether at work, a personal party or the like, and they may have insights for you on the service providers they have encountered along the way. Finally, whenever you participate in an event as an attendee, keep your eyes open and pay attention to the service providers for that event. Notice if they have done a good job at whatever their specialty is, and if you like what you see ask to talk with the on-site supervisor; let this person know who you are, ask for their business card and give them one of your business cards in return.

CHOOSE YOUR STAFF

Unlike suppliers who are in the business of working for multiple event planners in a given area, your staff might consist of individuals who work exclusively for you. Hiring a person to serve "in-house" is a much more personal working relationship where personalities can, and do, come into play, especially if the assistant you hire is recommended by a friend or family member.

Of course, there is no hard and fast rule that says you must hire an assistant, but if you feel it's necessary and will help your business operate more efficiently and effectively, do it. Just remember you will be paying for that person's time, which will have an effect on your own revenue. Additionally, by having one or more employees you will likely become subject to your state's worker's compensation laws and be required to purchase a worker's compensation insurance policy.

Another possibility that has grown rapidly in popularity is the hiring of what's known as a "virtual assistant." These are people who, like you, are operating their own business out of their own home, with a focus on providing services to handle the tasks normally handled by an in-house assistant. When I first started my business this option was not available, but I have been impressed with the possibilities so far and think it is well worth considering.

As with event services suppliers, there are plenty of places on the Internet where you can hire a virtual assistant; some are websites specializing in matching virtual assistants with people like you who need their services, while others are websites where individual assistants advertise and promote their services. A good choice for an event planning professional such as yourself is to find someone living in or near your community who can provide virtual services but also be available in person when needed to help you run events, interact with suppliers and vendors, and other such tasks.

In most cases you will communicate with your virtual assistant primarily via e-mail, instant message or even via video chat using a free service like Skype (www.skype.com). A good general Internet site for locating virtual assistants is www.another8hours.com, or there may be a local site in your region depending on where you live.

When it comes to hiring assistants though, there is one cardinal rule you absolutely must not violate, no matter what:

DO NOT HIRE FRIENDS OR RELATIVES

Have you ever heard the saying, "It's not personal, it's business"?   That is the phrase I want you to keep foremost in your head as the mantra you repeat over and over when looking to hire an assistant, virtual or otherwise. Remember this phrase especially when it comes to friends and relatives who want to work for you. Yes, it will hurt their feelings when they ask about a job and you respectfully say, "Sorry, I can't do it."

There is really no good way to consistently hold your friends and relatives accountable for their work performance because you have already established certain relationships and the dynamics of those relationships are difficult, if not impossible to change. Your older brother or sister will not take kindly to being told how to do something, nor will your best friend care to hear exactly why a mistake they made at an event has caused you to miss a contract obligation and resulted in you now having to refund part of a client's money, or worse, cost you future business from that particular client.

I realize it is true that some family businesses do work well for everyone involved, but I do not suggest you leap into this fire until you've had a chance to fully establish your business and make it successful. And trust me on this, you will fare much better during this process of becoming well-established if you do on your own while accessing the skills and experience of other people with whom you don't already have a personal or family relationship.

The best way to hire a person, whether a virtual assistant or flesh-and-blood individual for your own office, is to have them submit a job application. A standard, generic job application can be purchased at any office supply store, or you can find templates online for only a few dollars. Check with your state employment office as well to see if there is a specific job application they have approved for use within their jurisdiction. As with suppliers, it is completely acceptable to ask the person you are considering hiring for references and for you to call those references to make sure the person has been truthful.

The advantage of using standard applications is that they are objective and professional; they all ask for the same basic information and do not cross the boundaries into inappropriate questions that might cause you legal problems such as a "homemade" application might. By this I mean they allow you to know the person's education and experi-

ence as objective criteria to decide whether (a) they qualify for the job and (b) qualify for the interview.

You have to be very, very careful what you ask and
how you use the information obtained in applications to
hire someone. If you ask someone their age, for example,
and the person is an older individual whose application you
reject based on that factor, you can be sued. If you ask
whether someone is handicapped and deny them a job on
that basis, again you can be sued.

In another example, you do need to know whether an
applicant has been convicted of a serious crime because it
could affect your business operations. For instance, if someone admits to having a conviction for embezzling money
from an event planning business (or any business, for that
matter), it is unlikely that is your best candidate and you are
within your legal rights to choose not to hire that person.

The hiring process can be challenging and you will have
to make difficult decisions when you "screen" applicants.
Some people may seem really interesting but lack experience; others will have experience, but not in your area of
expertise. When hiring, you have to decide how much you
want to teach and how much you want someone to know
already. When you are starting out, you will more likely seek
people with the same exact experience you need to do the
job well and correctly. Once you've made inroads and have
a measure of success, then you can become a mentor.

The place to start screening applicants is when you place
the advertisement for the position. Be as clear as possible
in establishing a "profile" for your ideal candidate; this profile might include years of experience in whatever task you

are wanting done, a certain minimum level of education (like an accounting degree if you're advertising for a book-keeper), specific event planning experience, certain levels of computer proficiency and anything else that relates to the tasks and responsibilities you will assign to this person.

ABOVE ALL...

Don't stop looking until you find the right person who is the best assistant to fill the position.

When you advertise for help, you will almost always re-ceive a lot of responses from people desperate to get a job but who don't actually fit the profile to be your assistant. They are people you know nothing about except what they choose to tell you, so be very clear about your needs and draft as detailed a profile as possible.

THE IMPORTANCE OF WRITTEN AGREEMENTS

When hiring a person for a long-term position, a supplier for a specific function or event or even a hired hand for a just a day or two, it is critically important to put as many details as possible into writing. This contract will spell out in clear, concise language the details of things like what you expect the person to do, what you will pay that person, what their hours of work will be and other important provisions regard-ing dispute resolution and termination. It is very important that you go through this agreement with the person in de-tail and in advance to make sure they understand exactly what is expected of them. You can find employment contract templates online or you can purchase them at your local office supply store. I would not, however, suggest you draft one yourself unless you have an attorney review it prior to actually using it.

The reason this agreement is so important is that if something goes wrong with the employment, supplier or temporary relationship, you have a document you both discussed from the beginning that establishes everything about your professional working relationship. It lays out what you can and cannot do as an employer and what the person can and cannot do as an employee. There is a whole body of case law dedicated to this subject, so it is not a minor thing because to create that case law, people had to sue other people over what these agreements stated.

IMPORTANT

An employer-employee agreement is a serious thing and a binding legal document. Do not improvise and do not attempt to enter into any employer-employee relationship without one. If you don't have a good, solid agreement like this in place, it can very easily come back to hurt you in the end.

It is also wise to invest time and money in an employee handbook if you have more than one employee. These books lay out the contract terms but also include topics like health insurance, employee discipline, vacation time, sick time, and worker's compensation. Depending on the country and state in which you live, a handbook such as this might even be a legal requirement, so check with your state employment office for details.

KEEPING YOUR TEAM INTACT

Once you have hired an employee or signed on a supplier, you have an obligation to that person (or people) to treat them well and with respect. Nobody likes a tyrant for a boss, nor do they appreciate someone who is wishy-washy about communicating their expectations. Just as importantly, once you have put together a good team of people whose skills and talents contribute to the success of your business, you certainly do not want to risk losing them and having to go through the hiring process once again. Keeping your team intact, then, is not only the right thing to do from a professional perspective, but it is also the right thing to do from a business perspective as well.

Here are several areas to focus on in order to maintain good working relationships and be the kind of professional business owner with whom others want to do business:

- **Communication** - If the task is simple, say what you want in a manner that the average person can understand. Then, if you notice the person seems confused, say it again in a different way so that they understand what is expected of them. Sometimes you need to create task lists for a given day or even a memorandum. Check for understanding after you give instructions and make yourself available if the person has questions.

If an employee comes to you with questions, always respond to him or her with courtesy and respect no matter how silly you might think the question is or how many times you think you've already answered it. Remember, the respect you show your employees and associates will reflect on your business as a whole, and a good professional manner of communication will be a giant step towards developing and maintaining a positive business reputation.

It is best whenever possible to write down the things you want your assistant to do because it eliminates confusion and resolves the issue of wondering whether you directed that person to do something or not. This is called creating a paper trail and it is important because it protects you from liability and gives crystal clear directives to the employee. You will also have to use this technique when dealing with a virtual assistant.

Also, any communication that is related to employee discipline or terminating a contract with an associate, without exception, must be put in writing. Not only does this protect you, but it is almost always a legal requirement that must be followed.

Finally, make sure you conduct regular employee evaluations (in writing) so the person knows where they stand in light of your expectations for their work performance. This not only ensures both you and the employee have a clear understanding of what is expected, but it also allows the employee an opportunity to correct any problem areas and bring their performance up to your expectations.

- **Consistency** - This goes hand in hand with communication; however it is that you choose to communicate with an employee or associate, make sure you do so consistently. For instance, don't write down task assignments one day but then the next day only communicate them verbally. Also, never scream or raise your voice to an employee or associate; this is not only unprofessional but in some cases it could be in violation of certain workplace regulations as well. Do also give advance notice and adequate time for an employee to finish a difficult or more complicated task.

The more consistent and even-handed you are in dealing with the employee or associate, the better you will be perceived as an event planning professional and a business owner. Additionally, your services will have a consistency in delivery that will create confidence in the minds of your clients and more often lead to repeat business.

- **Recognition** – Everyone craves recognition, and in fact this is one of the most effective ways to reward good work and encourage employees to perform up to your expectations. If an employee or associate does an outstanding job, by all means recognize that achievement; many times a simple and sincere "thank you" is like music to the ears of an employee, or you can also reward good performance with a bonus, a gift card to a favorite restaurant, a certificate of achievement or an extended lunch at your expense.

The bottom line is that everyone likes to know they are appreciated and valued as well as that the work they have done is good, but, unfortunately, far too few employers take the time or make the effort to offer recognition and appreciation. Remember, the success of your business can quickly be compromised simply by failing to establish and maintain good employer-employee relations. But likewise, your success can be assured by honoring the people who help you climb that ladder of success with a simple act of sincere and timely recognition.

- **Compensation** - You are the only one who knows what you can afford to pay someone for their services; however, there are minimum wage laws that govern the minimum amount you can pay certain employees. For example, union workers must be paid a certain wage as dictated by their union contracts; the United States Federal Government has also set a "minimum wage" that every employer must pay their employees as a base hourly figure; and many states also have their own higher minimum wage levels that you are required to pay.

You might be able to afford to pay your employees a salary, but calculating the appropriate salary for the work done and for the area in which you live can be challenging. Fortunately, there is an excellent tool to help you with this process located at www.salary.com. This website makes it easy to calculate a salary range for your area depending on the job duties the person will carry out for you.

When you hire a third-party contractor like a supplier or virtual assistant, they have already established the hourly rate they will charge you and you must agree to it before retaining their services. Always double check your financial situation to ensure you can indeed cover this cost, and always make sure you pay on time the full amount owed, without exception and based on the contract of employment. Encourage continued good performance and create an incentive for that employee to remain with you as a valued part of your team.

- **Commissions** – In some situations, you might also hire people on a commission basis, meaning that what you pay them is determined by the amount of business they bring in. So, for example, if you hire a promoter to bring events to you he or she can be paid based on the number of referrals that actually result in you signing a client.

- **Share Options** - You can also offer an individual a stake in the business as an incentive to work in a start-up venture. Essentially, what this entails is creating an agreement with the person to accept a piece of your business pie. For example, let's say you meet someone who seems really interested in helping you, they apply for a position and you hire them. In exchange for their efforts to make your business work and assisting with certain day-to-day tasks, you give them a percentage ownership in the business. They then receive that percentage from every job you do successfully together.

All of the above are important pieces in establishing and maintaining good working relationships, but at the end of the day the best tools at your disposal are honesty, professional integrity and ethics. Without these three things you might as well give up right now. Remember, there are no shortcuts in creating employment relationships and if you decide to try one, believe me, you will be the sorry one in the end.

And I have some great news... I've got a few bonus gifts for you. Grab them online right now by joining my insiders list at www.MasteringEventPlanning.com.

CHAPTER RECAP

1. Creating a strong team is critical to ensure all necessary tasks are handled professionally, promptly and correctly. Consider using a contractor or temporary assistants if you are not ready to take on a direct employee.

2. Choose your suppliers carefully, using the Internet as a first tool for researching and finding possible suppliers. Interview each one carefully, check their references and determine if they are responsible, reliable and a good fit for your needs.

3. If you decide to hire an in-house staff member, approach the hiring process as you would any other critically important task. Interview potential people carefully and consider using a "virtual assistant" if that is a good fit for your needs. Check the employment laws for your city, town, state and/or country to ensure you are following them correctly. Finally, **NEVER** hire a friend or relative; it will create all sorts of problems and is never a good idea.

4. Always use written agreements, whether it's for an employee, a contractor, a vendor, a supplier or the like. This kind of agreement specifies all of the details of your business relationship, outlining responsibilities and accountabilities for all parties. Written agreements are your best protection against poor performance, giving you the leverage you need to hold everyone accountable for their designated tasks and roles.

5. Once you have put together a team of people, vendors and suppliers that work well, do what is necessary to keep that team intact. Treat them well and with respect and they will continue to give you their best efforts, creating a true win-win situation. Some key areas of focus should include:
- Communication
- Consistency
- Recognition
- Compensation
- Commissions
- Share options

CHAPTER 8

YOUR BUSINESS AND MARKETING PLAN

"He who fails to plan, plans to fail."

Proverb

THE BUSINESS PLAN

I'm going to start this chapter by telling you that every time a business is launched, the topic of the business plan will come up sooner rather than later. And regardless of who brings the topic to the table first—it could be your spouse, a friend, a lawyer, or potential business partner, just to name a few—at some point, they will ask to see your business plan to test whether you are really serious, capable and professional enough to do this business as an entrepreneur.

I personally believe a formal business plan for an initiative like starting your home-based event planning business, is a very complicated and usually unnecessary document. It is full of information you are simply not going to be able to put together accurately or in enough detail when first starting your business. That's because it's very difficult to look into the future of your own business to foresee and calculate all the information a regular business plan should include.

THE TRUTH IS...

Unless you are seeking formal bank or lending institution financing for seed capital, you don't need to write a formal business plan to start your event planning business.

Now, please don't misinterpret this statement; you **do** need to have a plan of action for your business.

But an outline of the activities necessary to kick start your business, such as identifying your niche and creating marketing materials, is completely different than writing a traditional, formal business plan. And when you are just starting out, if you spend the significant amount of time it takes to write a formal business plan, you will merely be doing a very good job of delaying the most important task you have to perform: selling.

I remember when I first started; I kept telling myself that I was going to do a formal business plan, wrongly believing that I needed one in order to be a "true" entrepreneur. The truth of the matter was though, that I could never find the time to sit down and write what I found to be such a boring document based on information which, at that point, was not very clear to me since I had zero experience in event planning and business management. So I threw my pen and paper away and ended up not writing a formal business plan when I started my business; instead, I wrote down a series of actions I knew I had to take in order to have my business sell its first events. This practice of putting in writing all of my ideas and plans for the immediate future became a practice for me and I still use this good habit to visualize my goals... and accomplish them.

After several years of being in business, however, I decided I wanted to write my company's business plan. I was finally ready. Even so, I did not have the time to dedicate to writing a good business plan, but I became obsessed with getting it done so I convinced two of my former employees to come to the office at 7:00 AM every morning for two full months to write and complete the infamous and dreaded business plan. Once complete, it was indeed useful and I'm not going to say it wasn't; it helped us make many decisions involving managing and marketing my business for quite some time, which was good.

But aside from that, and especially when you are just starting out, a business plan can only help you accomplish any one of these three things:

To get financing. But remember, no one is going to fund your home-based event planning business anyway. This may be hard to accept, but it's a hard reality because you are operating from your residence and not a commercial space. So, if you are not looking for money, or if you already know that no one is interested in your big and profitable business endeavor, don't waste precious and valuable time that could be much better spent capturing those first and crucial sales your new business so desperately needs.

To establish details about your future business goals. In other words, what direction do you want the business to take and what would you like to accomplish within certain benchmark time periods (six months, one year, five years, etc.)? Honestly though, because most of you have little to no experience whatsoever in event planning and because you're just starting out, you will simply not be able to clearly set goals or foresee appropriate benchmarks. That only comes once you gain some real life experience as an event planner; in fact, I would argue it is almost impossible when all you want to do is get your new business off the ground. You have to make real sales to real clients for real money, not dream about what might be down the road.

Besides, as I have said before, you can put in the effort to create a formal business plan after your business has been in operation for a few years, once you have gained some experience in your chosen event planning field. Don't forget, you might start out as a generalist, do it for a while and then decide you would rather be a specialist; or you might start out as a specialist and end up deciding to become a generalist.

So, the best case scenario would be to create a formal business plan once you gain some experience and know the data better, but in the beginning opt instead to informally create a general path to follow. Based on my experience, I can assure you that you don't need to invest all that time in writing a boring and useless business plan. Instead, I will tell you what might work much better for you later in this chapter.

When you are convinced you need to have one to start your business on the "right foot." Quite frankly, this will be your biggest obstacle to actually doing anything and working off this idea could indefinitely delay starting your new business because you most likely won't start writing it "just like that." I know most of the time people put off doing a business plan because it's extremely detailed, stressful and, at least to me, extremely boring. However, for some people the act of writing a business plan and having a detailed plan in place provides a certain level of comfort and security; while I still don't think it's necessary, if you fall into this category you might certainly feel you absolutely have to have one in order to move forward.

So, instead of drafting a traditional and useless business plan (and I mean it, which is why I deliberately keep using these words), I suggest you create a marketing plan instead. A marketing plan is a much simpler and more effective way to direct activities and progress for your home-based event planning business when you first start out; plus, it is a tool you can use throughout the time you run your business.

THE MARKETING PLAN

I want to begin this important section of my book by advising you to follow these three key principles in order to succeed in any business:

1. **Finish what you start.**   If you are reading this book, then you have probably already decided to start a new event planning business. Commit this to memory and do it; do it before you even start to think about the marketing plan. Never leave anything half done and always start from the beginning.

2. **Keep it simple.** When you draft your marketing plan, make sure you keep it simple. Simple is usable and sets achievable goals; complicated is not and does

not. Your marketing plan should be a simple and user-friendly document to which you can always refer when you need to make important decisions. Remember, your marketing plan is there in part to serve as your objective advisor for helping to make better decisions.

3. **Design it to win the business game.** Always create a marketing plan with the goal of playing this competitive event planning business game to win. To "win" means your marketing plan must focus on producing as much personal and business income as you can while also building as much value as possible for your clients.

FACT:

It is much better and more effective to set reasonable, practical, attainable goals, and then build on your successes as you move forward with your business.

Okay, let's get started with the real task at hand; that is, to start from the beginning and create an effective marketing plan. In this case, the beginning is where you establish your goals and then from there determine the best strategy to reach them one by one. Obviously then, it is useful to start by creating a list of these goals. Start with the most important but realistic goals you have in mind. You might be a bit curious about why I'm urging a certain amount of caution here at the start; after all, wouldn't it be better to establish some lofty, "reach for the stars" type of goals to inspire you toward success?

The answer to this question is, quite simply, no. No. No. Caution is a much more practical and useful approach at first because if you aim too high you will actually decrease your chances of success, not increase them. Why? Because goals that are too large, too pretentious and/or too far out of reach will more likely than not end up leaving you frustrated and discouraged because you are not getting anywhere close to accomplishing them.

But what, exactly, should these first few goals be? That's an easy one, and I've already given you the answer several times so far in this book. The first and most important goal to focus on when starting an event planning business (or really, any business) is to produce income. Nothing more, nothing less.

Therefore, your first goal should always be this big, broad, general one:

MAKE MONEY

All of the other goals you will ever set are inherently dependent on your ability to achieve this first goal, so they all come after the main reason you've chosen to start this business. It's also important to be clever and creative in setting your other goals with the underlying intent of producing income, period.

Start with small goals that can be accomplished in a shorter period of time; not too many, but enough to get you up and running. It could be something like: "Today I want my office space empty so I can start setting up all the furniture and have room for the supplies to start working by tomorrow." Or, "This week I will get the content for my website ready to send to my web programmer and upload my site."

Or, "This month I will visit at least 15 new potential clients to let them know about my services."

Don't get caught up in activities that appear to be productive but are not. For example, don't think attending another seminar, researching the Internet until late at night, reading another book, etc. will help you produce that necessary and desired income. If you want to make money, start doing sales-oriented tasks. I'm going to dedicate an entire chapter to this subject later in the book, but for now I will tell you that almost anything you do besides making money fast is a waste of time.

Of course, you will sometimes need to do other things unrelated to sales, but there's no one better than you to know if what you are doing is productive or not. So, go after productive tasks that are related to <u>actually producing money</u> rather than the more "planning to plan" tasks that are related to ideas and approaches you might try to produce money.

It is also critical to not be such a perfectionist that you can't take the next step in your marketing plan. In fact, I would go so far as to say forget all about being a perfectionist because that doesn't help put money in your pocket. Get the job done the best you can, but don't wait until you have the perfect business card or logo designed to "pull the trigger" and start selling. It is a waste of time and money to tweak and adjust and revise while you wait to get all your ducks in a row. Move on, put yourself out there and let everybody know you are in business and they can hire you to plan their next event.

Remember, you will always have extra time down the road to improve and adjust the things you are doing in the beginning. In fact, that will occur naturally simply as a result of building a solid, constant stream of income from your business, but not before.

You will also want to set bigger goals to accomplish over the next slightly longer time period, let's say six months to one or two years. These mid-to long-term goals could be something like, "In six to 12 months I will have full-time income from my business by selling my services on a regular basis"; or, "In two years my annual sales and revenues will be this or that number," depending on your specific activity within the event planning industry. As with all goals though, be direct, be specific and be realistic. And yes, always keep aiming higher, one goal at a time.

Finally, after creating your marketing plan, go back through it and change your goals into real, specific promises. Why? Because you are far more likely to hold yourself accountable to your promises than to your goals, since a promise is a personal commitment to do something. Not fulfilling that promise would damage your integrity, something which I know you are absolutely not willing to let happen.

YOUR DESIRED RESULTS DETERMINE YOUR STRATEGY

As I have already said, the easiest and most effective way to plan for your business is to first set the desired, realistic goals you want to accomplish, whether they are short term, medium term, or long term. Secondly, develop a real and specific strategy to accomplish and achieve each of these goals.

For example, let's say you establish a goal of getting one new paying client each month over the next 12 months. As a strategy to accomplish that goal, you could commit to make at least five appointments with potential clients every week and respond to every sales inquiry in 24 hours or less. This would naturally lead you to follow up regularly on all leads and become flexible in providing customized alternatives and solutions to potential clients in order to convert them to actual paying clients.

Let's simplify this even further. When you're putting together your business and marketing strategies, remember this one thing:

The essence of successful event planning business strategy is to buy or create something and then sell it to your client at a profit.

Taking it another step further, in every business, including yours, there are three universal areas of focus:

1. Marketing

2. Production

3. Operations

In these first early stages you should focus primarily on marketing. Why? Because this is where the money is and without it you will have no clients and, consequently, no revenue. Production consists of buying or creating the product you are selling, and operations mainly involve administration and finances as well as the delivery of the item.

Therefore, you must start this business with the mindset that you are in the marketing and sales business, not the event planning business, so you should be skilled (or quickly develop the skills needed) at both. A good rule of thumb to follow in determining how to divide your time and energy among these three areas of focus is as follows:

- Marketing - 60%

- Production – 20%

- Operations – 20%

Let me reiterate, if you want to become a successful entrepreneur, you need to focus your attention on revenue, cash flow, and profit rather than on income alone, which is what most people mistakenly first assume. Remember, without adequate revenue, cash flow and profit you will never have a decent personal income; this means you consistently have to design your marketing strategy and plan so you realize greater revenues, higher cash flow, higher profit margins and lower expenses.

Why am I so adamant on this issue? It comes from personal experience, or should I say, personal mistakes. You see, these are the mistakes I made with regard to this issue and my goal here is to help make sure you don't make the same mistakes I did.

Looking back, I remember at one point my only concern, as it is with most people, was to produce revenue for my business; and I was actually very good at it. Every month I was closing more and more sales for events, but I forgot to pay attention to the importance of increasing my profits, generating higher cash flow and simultaneously keeping my expenses low. At some point, everybody in my company, including myself, was working so hard you can't even imagine what a nightmare I had created for myself and for all of us. We were working double shifts, traveling every week, literally leaving our souls in the job; but as a company, we weren't making enough money. Despite the fact that there had never been a busier time in my career... we weren't profitable.

It was my fault that we found ourselves in this situation because I lost control of the numbers until I realized that I was forgetting the importance of focusing my attention on revenue, cash flow, lower expenses and income, instead of only revenue. So I urge you, I'm pleading with you, to never allow yourself to lose control of those numbers like I did. Recognize what work and effort is profitable and what is not, and then, obviously, only focus on the profitable tasks and businesses.

*Learn how to say "NO" to jobs from which you
will earn no profit.*

IMPORTANT

Never work for free as that will kill your business faster than you might ever think is possible.

These are the most difficult two letters to combine and say to a client, so practice: "NO." Of course you need to have cash flow, but realize that not all income is profit and oftentimes bad business means income losses. So, be aware of your numbers and focus your energy and resources on activities you can profit from; do not sell your services just for the sake of selling. If you follow this approach, then you can be certain you are getting your increased revenues and cash flow while also decreasing expenses.

What does all of this really mean? Let's put it into actual numbers in an actual example.

Suppose you want your business to make $100,000 in profit each a year; in order to reach this goal you have to understand exactly what it will take to get there. Here is what I have found to be the simplest way and a good general strategy to follow:

- If you sell $100,000 net in events

- And you realize a 20% profit from that $100,000

- You need $500,000 in gross sales per year to reach that $100,000 net profit

Your strategy then, should answer these two critical questions:

1. What do I need to do to sell $500,000.00 in events a year?

2. What specific steps will I take to reach that goal?

There you have it. You're ready to go, so make a list of tasks and go for it. You have already calculated and know you have to generate $500,000 a year in sales, which sounds like a huge dollar figure but in this business believe me, it is not all that difficult. You merely have to focus on sales and excel in your performance as an event consultant and specialist. That means putting yourself out there, offering your services and following up consistently and persistently until you close the deal. Then take the steps necessary to make sure you end up with a happy client (and thus very likely a return client).

In this case, you can break down your annual goal further; to reach it, and only as an example, you need to sell 25 event contracts per year at $20,000 each. And always remember, right along with increasing your revenues, increasing your cash flow and increasing your profit margins, it is vitally important to keep your expenses low if you want to have a successful business.

KEEP IT SIMPLE

As you continue to work through writing your marketing plan, remember this next crucial component:

KEEP IT SIMPLE

How can you do this? I suggest you ask yourself the following questions:

1. **What product or service you will provide, what's the solution you deliver, and what problem do you solve so clients will want to pay you for a solution when organizing an event?**

Respond to this question in 20 words or less. In my case, I offer clients the possibility to dream their fantasy special event and actually bring their ideas into reality, since we have developed the capability to produce just about anything a customer requires for an event, adding a touch of greatness and awe. Remember, be clear and concise; if you confuse your clients about your services, they won't remember how you can help them solve their problems.

2. Who is your target audience?

It may sound obvious, but remember this: if you don't know who your potential clients are or where to find them, you probably will not be able to get to them and win their business. It's like they say, "If you can't define them, you can't find them."

REMEMBER....

The more specifically you define the person (i.e. the potential client), the better and more easily you can find and serve them.

In my opinion, it is better to have a very specific and focused target audience rather than one which is huge and broad. Why? There are a couple of reasons. First, the greater the number of people you're marketing to, the greater your marketing costs will be, but this increase in costs does not necessarily translate to marketing results that are more productive and more profitable. Second, the smaller and more targeted the people are to whom you are marketing, the more effective your marketing efforts will be and the more productive and profitable your results will be.

This means you have to study all the information you have at hand about your entire potential audience in order to better segregate and narrow things down to your target audience. This can be done by examining age, gender, geography, income, marital status, education, lifestyle, buying, professional profile, habits, etc. And it is always good to keep in mind that some of the best prospects are those who have already bought the products and/or services you are selling (even if it was from a competitor) or something similar.

Therefore, if I sell special event services, then my target audience will be people who have bought my products in the past whether from my business or from a similar and competing business. In my case, this audience can be described as follows:

- Executives employed by large domestic and international corporations

- Most have college degrees

- Many have postgraduate education

- Male or female

- Aged between 28 and 50 years old

- They are the decision makers

- They are in charge of their company's event planning department

- They are marketing, sales, human resources and public relations executives

- They are responsible for hiring the providers needed for any particular gathering, event or activity

- They may be business owners, sales executives from meeting planning companies, hotels and/or convention centers

- And this list can go on and on

What's more, our individual clients always tend to want to get the best deals; and they are very familiar, if not experts, in what they do; therefore, they have "seen it all" and are constantly seeking to be surprised or positively impressed with new creative ideas and innovation.

Can you see how these kinds of very detailed, specific descriptions allow me to narrow down my target audience so that I can focus my efforts on those people who are most likely to need and want my services? If you do the same kind of thing for your event planning business, then you will be well on your way to attracting more clients and growing your business by leaps and bounds.

3. How will your target audience find you?

You need to know the specific steps and tasks necessary to familiarize your target market with your business. In other words, you have to get them to know that you exist. There are a number of ways to accomplish this, such as:

- Personal calls and appointments

- Word of mouth

- Referrals

- The Internet

- E-mail campaigns

- Organizing one or two events in your community to promote your brand

- Placing ads in a targeted magazine or publication

So, which of these tactics should you use? I can't answer that specifically because your event planning business is unique, but what I would recommend is that you use an integrated media plan that encompasses one or more of these outreach methods in whatever combination is best suited to your business needs. You should never rely on one method, but neither should you start with a full array of five, six, seven or more methods all at once. Instead, choose those methods that are most likely to reach your target audience and that fit your available marketing budget.

In short, never underestimate the power of well-chosen advertising and marketing to promote your business and get noticed. It really works and is very useful for attracting new clients to your door.

4. Is there a market for the particular event planning service you are considering?

The easiest way to discover if there is indeed a market for your proposed service is to see if you already have competition. Not having any competition doesn't necessarily mean there isn't a market, but it is not necessarily a good sign either. Search the Internet, review the yellow pages and check the classified ads in the newspaper to determine whether there's a market or not. When you are dealing with special event services, I don't think it is possible not to have a market at all, but at the same time you need to make sure there is enough of a market within your chosen niche for your business to be profitable and sustainable.

5. What will make you stand out from the competition?

Don't be so vague and ambiguous as to say you will be the best event planner. That literally means nothing. It is better to assert you are the best fundraising event specialist in your area or the event planner that organizes the most elegant events. My company is distinguished from the competition by asserting: "We organize spectacular and enjoyable events." My clients know that if they need a spectacular event at which people will have the time of their lives, they can call us to do the job.

However, if my client wants the most elegant and classy event possible, I wouldn't necessarily be the best one to call. Yes, my events might be spectacular and certainly enjoyable, and of course my company is able to produce elegant settings, but there are other companies out there that specialize precisely in creating classical-elegant events, very refined, and simply that is not my specialty. This is a very effective assertion and I use it every single day to help define and focus my business efforts.

Remember, your Unique Selling Proposition should answer these two questions: "Why should I buy it?" And then, "Why should I buy it from you?" Be careful not to establish a USP that your target audience doesn't care about; also remember, your USP doesn't come from being a master of made-up words to please someone. Instead, it must be driven by the client's needs and your skill set. Ask yourself every time:

What does your client want? And then deliver it to him in the form of a USP.

6. What will your overhead cost be?

I cannot emphasize enough how important it is to try to keep your costs low, but by the same token you would be completely wrong to assume that you won't have overhead costs just because you work from home and work on your own. It doesn't matter how big your business is or where it operates from, it will have overhead costs. So, don't ignore every little or big expense you need to properly run your business, but instead consider everything from fuel costs, phone bills, cell phone bills, electricity and every other kind of material you will use that can be included in that overhead cost.

7. How much time are you willing or able to work every day and week?

Be as honest as possible with yourself about this number, but also be aware that the reality of owning and running your own business is often somewhat different than you might expect going into it. It is not uncommon for a new small business to sometimes require you to put in a lot of hours a day for many days in a row if you truly want it to take off and succeed.

8. How much income do you need to pay your bills, and can your new business provide you with that?

Owning your own event planning business is a great way to establish what your work is really worth. However, sometimes (especially in the beginning) having a business means sacrificing a great deal of time and freedom to do other things that you like in order to create the opportunity to make more money than you otherwise would in a regular 40-hour-per-week job.

Every now and then I share new tricks and tips that I discover while on the event planning trenches... If you'd like to find out what those are and stay up to date on this topic, become an insider at www.MasteringEventPlanning.com

CHAPTER RECAP

1. Although conventional wisdom says you must create a business plan to be successful, in my experience a business plan is a complicated and unnecessary document. The only reason you would need to write a formal business plan is if you intend to seek financing from a bank or other lending institution. If you are not going this route then don't waste your time or energy writing a business plan.

2. Instead, you are much better off creating a specific and detailed marketing plan for your event planning business. This plan should be in line with three key principles necessary for success:
- Finish what you start
- Keep it simple
- Design it to win the business game

Start with the most important goal of all: MAKE MONEY. Your marketing plan should begin with small, measurable, achievable steps designed to reach reasonable goals in a shorter period of time. The idea is to get your business up and running. Then you can move on to intermediate time frame goals, followed by long term goals. Throughout this entire process, the overall goal remains the same: MAKE MONEY. And you do this by mapping out and taking real, concrete actions.

3. Establish your desired results and then develop the specific strategy necessary to achieve those results. Remember, your desired results are what determine your strategy, not the other way around. And the most basic of all desired results is to provide a product or service to your clients, selling it to them at a profit.

4. Pay attention to the three universal areas of business focus, dividing your time and energy as follows:
- Marketing – 60%
- Production – 20%
- Operations – 20%

Underlying all of these efforts is the first and foremost need of any business; that is, to focus on revenue, cash flow and profit, not on income alone.

5. Choose your clients and jobs carefully, taking only those from which you can make a reasonable profit. Learn how to say "NO" to jobs from which you will earn no profit.

6. As you work through your marketing plan, KEEP IT SIMPLE. Ask and answer questions such as:
- What product/service/solution of value to clients do you deliver?
- Who is your target audience?
- How will your target audience find you?
- Is there a real market for the type of service you plan to deliver?

- What will make you stand out from the competition?
- What will your overhead costs be?
- How much time are you willing/able to work?
- How much income does your new business need to provide to pay your bills?

CHAPTER 9

EVENT PREP, PLANNING, AND EXECUTION

"It is no use saying 'We are doing our best.'
You have got to succeed in doing what is necessary."

-- Winston Churchill, former Prime Minister of Great Britain

In this chapter, I will outline the activities and steps necessary to help you organize, conduct and/or coordinate a flawless event, thereby guaranteeing its success.

No matter the size or location of your event, basic event management uses the same skills and procedures in terms of actions and activities that need to be undertaken.

Although this detailed list makes it appear as if these activities are done in "chronological" order, in fact, many of them should be undertaken at the same time. In order to have a better understanding of this progression as a whole,

I'm going to divide the event management process into three different phases: before, during and after the event.

BEFORE: PRE-EVENT PLANNING

Before pulling together all the pieces that make up an event, you must spend time gathering crucial information necessary to both begin and successfully complete the production process. I call this "forward thinking" because an event really does have a beginning, middle and a conclusion or end. To make the whole event a wonderful experience, you have to keep all the segments of activity in mind from the very beginning. It requires gathering all crucial information from the client, including background details about the event as well as the goals and objectives of the event.

Therefore, when I meet a client either face-to-face or speak to him/her on the phone to discuss actually organizing an event, I always make sure to find out the following information:

1. Where will the event take place?

This is probably one of the first questions you should ask when planning an event, but it is not uncommon for the answer to be "I don't know" or "To be determined." Although not having this answer right up front may make it difficult to make other important decisions involved in the design and production process, you still have a bit of "wiggle room" in which to get a final answer to this question. You can still move forward and create your project, leaving this answer for later, as long as you come back to this question as a high priority decision to be made.

2. What kind of event are we talking about?

This question begins to get at the purpose, goals and objectives of the event as defined by the client. So, for instance, it should be obvious that a corporate anniversary probably calls for an elegant venue of some significance to the corporation, like a museum or gallery, while a new product launch would more likely take place in a hotel ballroom, convention center, auditorium or other similar venue.

When you understand what kind of event the client wants and the goals and objectives that he is pursuing, know the nuances of where a particular client will feel most comfortable and identify where the event can be held to present best to the client's target audience, you will be well on your way to gaining many new clients because you'll know how to "get it right." However, if you don't pay enough attention to this question and you "get it wrong," it could very easily (and very likely) end up costing your clients in the future. Never, ever forget that the event planning business is as much about word-of-mouth in your selected specialty as traditional advertising and promotion.

3. Who is the event for, how many attendees are we expecting, what percentage of attendees are male and what percentage of attendees are female?

Knowing the answers to these questions determines the direction you will take in designing your event. This includes what you will suggest for decorations, what you will recommend for entertainment, and many other issues surrounding identification and selection of an appropriate venue and theme.

4. When will the event take place?

This is a critical question for sure, but in many cases it might not be something the client can respond to immediately and definitively. It is better to prepare for the very real likelihood that the "when" of the event will be determined later on (often much later on) into the planning process. At the very least, however, you should be able to get from your client some sort of guesstimate or "ballpark" time for the event, such as "spring," "December," "after 2nd quarter," or the like.

5. What is the client's real, actual budget (not the "wish list" or "maybe" budget)?

I cannot emphasize enough how important it is to know your baseline budget figures; this means, know what money is actually "in the bank" and allocated to the event specifically. It's fine for a client to "think" he or she might be able to come up with extra cash to add certain special items at some point, but you can never count on this actually happening. What's more, in the event industry the prices of services are wildly diverse, so you really have to give yourself and the client a reality check early on with regard to the true costs involved in order to avoid potential overruns.

For example, you can book one type of entertainment for a gala dinner for a budget of $2,000 or a different type of entertainment for a budget of $5,000. The same applies to venues, catering, DJ's, decorations, equipment, and the list just goes on and on. But it's the amount of money that your client actually has to spend which will dictate how you allocate the available budget among the different types (and prices) of services available.

This is absolutely critical because you need to balance the real, actual budget against all of the client's needs, not just one small part. You have to determine the budget for each concept and the total budget for the event overall, allowing you to then come up with the combination of the right solutions at the right price.

It has been my experience that some clients have no problem letting you know their budget, but that others will really resist divulging this information up front. Their reasoning is often that they believe they will receive a better price from you by remaining silent about the true budget, on the assumption that if they tell you the true amount then you are going to figure out a way to charge them everything they have set aside for the event. It's simply human nature to toss a coin in the hope of getting a better deal; if they don't tell you the true budget, then they think it's likely you will end up charging them less overall.

REALITY CHECK

This sort of game playing can and will happen to you so don't be surprised when it comes along; in fact, you need to be prepared for it and just assume it will happen so you can be in a better position to address the issue and plan your time accordingly.

As should be obvious, this is simply nonsense. What on earth is a budget for if not to form the baseline off of which you plan the event in the first place? Clients often tell me they simply don't have a specific budget for the event or a particular service and that they want to see my price quote for the event as described first. My experience has taught me that this is not a very helpful method of planning an event and creating a successful outcome, and also that this kind of answer (i.e. they don't have a budget set aside) is nearly always not true.

And, not surprisingly, 90% of the time when I submit a pro-posal without knowing the budget up front, this clever client will tell me the price is far too high and they need to see lower priced alternatives. At that point, I think to myself that if I had known their budget to begin with, we wouldn't be starting all over again, revising all the services to come up with a lower price. As you can well imagine, this is extremely frustrating and expensive because when that happens, you have already spent time preparing a full proposal or even a simple quote, only to end up revising every single item on it and working double time to deliver again.

The answers to these five questions listed above will dictate the details and actions for you to take during the production process. Additionally, getting a clear understanding of the event as a whole in the beginning will serve as a guide you can follow to get things done and make the best decisions throughout the whole process of pulling your event together.

Okay, what comes next?

Once the general and broad brushstrokes of the "where, when and why" questions have been addressed, you need to delve into the more detailed questions that are also criti-cal to ask right in the beginning, the most obvious of these being issues related to the guests. Why? Because who your guests are influences a number of different factors and out-comes that, like before, will influence and determine a num-ber of critical event planning choices.

For instance, think for a moment about invitations. These can take a huge variety of forms, ranging from an email to a fancy engraved invitation to a themed invitation and more. You need to understand both the importance of selecting the most appropriate type of invitation for your event sticking to the allotted budget, and of having a reliable registration system in place to gather and record as much information as possible about your guests.

When organizing larger events, you can set an efficient registration system in place to record the responses and preferences of attendees. Some examples of things to be captured and noted include:

- Selection of workshops to attend

- Food preferences

- Payment options

- Accommodations

- Options for including family in the event activities

- Directions to and from the event location

The particular event registration system you put in place needs to be able to track and record answers to these key questions, but the client also needs to have a clear understanding of why these questions (and these answers) are so critical to the event planning process.

For instance, you should review with the client questions such as the following:

1. Will most of your guests attend with their families?

This is important because entertainment options for the event are largely based on the average age of the attendees or guests. If children will be present, then the entertainment should be attractive and appropriate for them; if the audience for entertainment will be adults, however, then the entertainment needs to appeal more to adult tastes and preferences.

Another thing to take into consideration when children will attend is the menu. Kids generally don't like to eat the same kinds of food as adults, so in addition to the regular menu it's a good idea to also have plenty of "kiddie" food available as well. And here's a valuable tip to keep in mind: it's very common for adults to prefer this "kiddie" food as well, so plan to serve it in enough quantities to satisfy the number of children expected plus some extra for those adults as well.

2. Will the guests be mostly men, mostly women, or an even balance of the two genders?

As mentioned above, the answer to this question will influence many things such as the decorations, giveaways, entertainment, and other amenities. For instance, when the majority of guests are going to be female, we emphasize the table settings and floral arrangements, as well as the decorations and overall ambience. Perhaps not surprisingly, when the male guests will outnumber female guests, we emphasize food, beverages, entertainment and giveaways more, because these are the things that males tend to notice and enjoy the most.

3. How many guests will be attending?

The number of guests your client is expecting will determine the size of the location, the amount of food to be served, the type and quantity of entertainment and many other things. Keep in mind that there is a direct correlation between the number of guests and the menu options you can offer. If it is a large crowd, you will have to make sure that whatever entertainment is selected is set up so that it can be seen and heard equally by everyone. And of course, most event venues have a legal capacity limit by which you'll have to abide as well. So, you wouldn't want to hold a wedding reception for 250 people in a venue where the legal capacity is only 200, any more than you would hold a Christmas party for a small business with 100 people in a convention center ballroom with a capacity of 500.

4. Are your guests primarily couples or singles?

If you are hosting couples on an incentive trip, for instance, they probably will want to dance at the farewell dinner. That means you will have to retain a band that plays dance music. But if the guests are mostly singles or attendees coming to the event alone, then another type of entertainment might suit them better, like games or any kind of interactive entertainment like a TV-style "game show" or karaoke. Likewise, in terms of food, the couples might prefer a three-course plated dinner to encourage conversation, while single people might prefer buffet stations that help stimulate circulation throughout the room and the initiation of new conversations.

5. What is the average age of the guests?

Knowing the average age of your guests will help you find and retain the right entertainment alternatives. For example, you probably don't want to have a couple of tango dancers at a children's festival or a classical violinist at a Sweet Sixteen birthday party.

6. Do the guests know each other?

When people attending an event already know each other, such as co-workers or related families, you can offer different types of interactive entertainment than if your guests don't know each other already. When people are already acquainted, they might just want pure entertainment that offers something new or different from what they are used to; on the other hand, people who are primarily strangers might prefer something that allows them to interact more with each other and help them make new friends.

7. Are the guests from the local community or are they from out of town?

When guests are coming from out of town, you probably want to choose a location that is easy to find. And if, for example, there will be a giveaway of some sort, make sure the items are something they can travel with easily on the return trip home. It also makes sense to host your event near or in a place they can stay, such as a hotel with special event or conference rooms.

8. Do the guests work for the same company?

If your guests are co-workers, nothing works better than entertaining them with interactive activities, games, and dynamic activities related to teambuilding in which they can participate without the risk of being embarrassed.

9. Can you profile your guests?

More often than not, some events are for certain types of people that tend to like certain things as a group. For example, some groups enjoy interactive events instead of merely watching a show. Others prefer fancy venues and an elegant setting rather than a relaxed and casual ambience that another, more laidback group might prefer.

To show how important this can be to help make your event a success, I will tell you a personal story from when we planned events for a corporate client. Being highly creative people overall, the group always wanted an outside-the-box concept for their annual corporate event. On one occasion, we organized a "talent night" where they could perform singing, dancing, acting or even playing an instrument... something that highlighted whatever their artistic skill might be. The only catch was they had to imitate a famous artist or play. It was a huge success and an event they never forgot.

REMEMBER...

If you can profile your guests for a certain event, it will help you decide many things like the ideal location, entertainment, interactivity levels, menu and other such things with more accuracy and ease.

We provided another client with all the accessories and necessary equipment for each of the guests to create their own painting. It was such a hit and the results were so terrific that some of the paintings created during that event were taken back to the company headquarters where they hung on the walls for quite a few years. And the list goes on.

However, there is no such thing as a "sure thing" when it comes to setting up these kinds of activities based on guest profiles. That's why it's important to have a good idea in advance of things that might go wrong and have a contingency plan in place "just in case."

In the example of the paintings, for instance, we were worried about what would happen if the guests were reluctant to step forward and take part in the painting activity. To deal with this possibility, we had a contingency plan in place where we arranged in advance with a few willing volunteers that they would "step up" and take an active role if one of our staff members felt the participation level was not taking off like we anticipated. It turns out we didn't have any problems with this, but it was good to have the back-up plan in place and ready to go just in case.

Putting a contract in place

Let's assume now that you already have an event confirmed and you have reviewed with the client the guest profiles and details. The very first thing you have to do is to make sure you and your client are on the same page about all of these issues and items by providing a formal, detailed contract for the client to sign.

Having this contract prepared and ready to go for signing not only makes you look more professional and organized, but it also establishes the scope of the project and your respective obligations, as well as protecting both parties from liability should either fail to carry out one or more of the obligations in the contract.

As stated in Chapter 4, I strongly suggest you create a basic contract format that you can use as a template, one for clients and one for vendors/service providers. Or you can go to one of the many online web pages for legal advice (www.legalzoom.com, www.lawguru.com or www.legaladviceline.com in the United States) where you will find a number of operative formats and documents, as well as sample contracts you can adapt to your specific needs and start using from day one.

When signing a contract with either clients or vendors, you must make sure you include information about critical details such as:

- Exactly what the service will include

- Payment terms

- How many people are included as staff

- The schedule for loading in and loading out

- How much time is needed for set-up

- Your specific requirements to provide the service

- Any extra charges that may apply

- Cancellation policies

This is a pretty good start to the list of what should be included in a good contract, but there are many, many more items you can (and probably should) put in there as well. As a general rule of thumb, you should try to include as much useful information in the contract as you can without getting into a "cold" and impersonal work agreement that is too bogged down in legalese. Too much legalese (terms used by lawyers and courts) that is put in there solely to protect you tends to scare clients away.

Instead, it is much better to spell out important terms like the ones mentioned in the preceding paragraph using plain, clear, everyday language that is easily understood by everyone involved. If the project is not huge or complicated, then it's usually enough to get a solid deposit and, if possible, payment in full before the event starts or a few days after. Then it is up to you to do an excellent job so your client will want to retain your services again in the future and/or recommend your services to others.

However, the obvious exception to this general rule is when you are signing "big" contracts involving large dollar amounts or more complex arrangements involving, say, unions for actors, laborers or musicians. In these more complicated situations, it is vital to make sure you get better and stronger legal protection.

IMPORTANT

Once you have a contract written up, the next step is to review it thoroughly.

The contract will allow you to start making decisions aimed at bringing every piece of the puzzle together per the terms of that contract so you must make sure it is accurate and complete. That way you will not find yourself liable for not doing something you should have or incurring costs for doing more than was required. This kind of attention to detail is called going the extra mile to make sure you get it right the first time.

Start with the payment provisions. It is important to understand that in order to start working on any project (no matter how big or how small) you will definitely need to get some money from the client up front. Never, ever agree to finance anyone's event; by "finance" I mean paying for services from your own pocket and then expecting reimbursement from the client. Please be aware that such concessions on your side could be devastating to your business if the client for any reason delays payment, reduces payment, or decides to withhold payment; this is especially true when you are first starting out.

I offer this advice because you will encounter a nearly infinite number of clients who will ask you to finance their events in this way. What's more, they will offer a thousand reasons why you should agree to do this, all of which sound perfectly wonderful and good. They may promise to give you a check for the full amount at the end of the event or have a wire transfer done on a certain day, the very day of the event or right after.

In all honesty, I don't care whether they promise to pay you one or two days before, on the day of the event or afterwards; I heartily encourage you not to accept such disadvantageous terms because without getting any money up front you are effectively servicing their debt (with no interest charges). This works totally against your interest in making a profit, and furthermore, let there be no doubt that clients failing to pay as promised can damage your business to the point where you'll have to quit before you even get started.

Do you think this sounds mean or "cold"? If so, ask yourself this: Why should you be the one to pay for anybody else's event? Perhaps it is just because they are giving you the "chance" to work for them when you are first starting your new business, but I need you to recognize that this is completely unacceptable and utter nonsense. The client decided to work with you, to choose you from among many others because they considered you to be the best alternative to have the best event possible. They are not doing you a favor; they are making a deliberate business decision to engage your services.

In other words, they are paying for something valuable to them too. In return, you offer every single item described in your agreement, most of which probably has a lot of added value to it. This should make it clear that the equation is fair (equal), and in this light it should no longer make sense to you to even consider financing any client's event, whether it's a company, individual, or family member.

Please, DON'T.

It's not fair to you and won't do your business any good. In fact, it will create the impression that you are a pushover, which is definitely not good for you or your business over the long run.

The reality is that accepting these kinds of unfavorable terms places you at their mercy. And also realize that if they didn't think it was fair for you to collect a down payment, or even your total payment up front, chances are they might become suspicious that something about your service is not as they think it should be even though everything is fine. It is highly likely that this type of client will try to find every reason imaginable (and then some) to adjust the amount of money they owe you in order to pay you less money overall.

And there's absolutely nothing you can do about it.

Of course you should always provide impeccable service if you want to keep your clients happy and your business going, but that most definitely does not mean accepting payment conditions that put you and your business at risk. So, no matter what anyone says, don't let them confuse you by mixing these two concepts of good service and payment. If you ask me, you should be paid in full before the event even starts, but in the real world it is far more common for 50% to be paid up front, with the balance becoming due immediately after the event ends. This kind of arrangement avoids most of the problems discussed above.

Review the contract terms carefully

Of course, you should know exactly what's in the contract prior to signing it, but once the down payment or full payment is deposited in your business account, you should review every clause of your contract again because now you actually have to perform your obligations. I suggest you use these clauses to create an event timeline, helping you to envision everything that needs to occur during that time period and to ensure you completely fulfill your obligations.

REMEMBER...

Make sure you do your timeline in such a way that planning the event feels neither rushed and frantic nor too slow and boring.

When I create a timeline, I always try to be as realistic as possible. When you're just starting out it helps to consider the fact that you are starting this event from zero, at the bottom. Think of yourself as taking what amounts to a "cold" audience, and make it your job to build every moment of the event so that when people leave at the event's conclusion, the magic factor has risen in crescendo until you reach the grand finale that leaves the guests wanting more and talking about the event for quite a long time.

Remember, you have the ability to plan an event that the guests and the client will remember literally forever. And that will translate into more new business and repeat business for you in the future.

Can you manage the event by yourself?

As you're reviewing the contract terms and obligations, pay close attention to the full scope of the event's requirements. Based on these details, can you manage the event yourself or will you need to bring in additional help?

Whether you can manage an event by yourself or not depends on the size and complexity of that event or project. If you already have a staff on hand, you might not have to hire additional help, but if not you might need to hire other vendors or temporary staff for a fixed period to help with the managing and coordination of the event.

Before you meet with any client, I would suggest you have every contingency covered: a plan for managing any event alone, with your staff on hand and with additional hired third parties. As discussed in Chapter 7, do your research ahead of time to find skilled professionals to help you manage events as you need them. In other words, in the beginning it's a good idea to have coordinators help you when you have more work than you can handle. You can look for freelancers instead of hiring them as your employees.

Put together an accurate and detailed timeline

After deciding the initial scope of the event, you can move forward and create a preliminary event timeline. But remember, nothing is set in stone; this preliminary plan can (and probably will) change significantly on your way to creating a final timeline.

The timeline is critical to have because from day one it will dictate how to properly negotiate with any other supplier involved in your production, including the entity providing the venue. It also helps you schedule every activity you have to carry out prior to and during the event. In general terms then, it provides you with a picture of when everything involved in this planning and putting on an event starts and ends.

When creating a timeline, you should ask yourself questions like:

- **On what day of the week will the event happen?** The day of the week will help you determine the time the event starts and ends. This, in turn, allows you to fill in the blanks and organize everything required within that time frame. An event that takes place on a Wednesday in the middle of the work week, for example, will not have the same duration as one that happens on a Friday or on a Sunday. In short, all three days should be managed differently.

For instance, on Wednesday you could start at 7 or 8 PM, which allows guests enough time to arrive after work, and then finish the event by 11 PM or midnight at the latest. But on a Friday or Saturday you could start the event later in the evening, allowing guests plenty of time to get dressed and made up for the event, and then not finish it until midnight, 1 AM, or even 2 AM if you like, since most people likely won't have to get up early the next day. If the event is to be held on a Sunday, you might want to consider arranging it as a lunch-to-dinner activity, ending it by 6 PM or so. Or, if you really prefer to offer dinner on a Sunday, you can ask your guests to arrive as early as 5 PM, serve dinner at 7 PM and then end the night at 10 PM at the latest.

- **What are you serving at the event?** What you decide to serve at the event influences everything from space needs to staffing needs to food needs and more. For instance, if you are having a cocktail hour with hors d'oeuvres, then you need to arrange for items such as tall cocktail-style tables, enough beverage servers to accommodate the expected number of guests, and most likely enough roaming servers and wait staff to circulate through the room with hors d'oeuvres trays. Or, if you are serving a plated dinner you will need regular dining tables, chairs, linens, silverware, centerpieces and, of course, servers to bring out the food and remove dirty plates. A buffet-style dinner requires many of these same things, but with more of a focus on staff to keep the buffet stocked. Always consider the space needed within the room to set up the buffet, allow for lines of guests waiting to be served and provide enough wait staff to clear dirty plates from around the room.

- **Will the guests be moving from one point to another within the parameters of your venue?** If this is the case, then you need to pay attention to the physical layout of the room and the likely traffic patterns people will follow as they move throughout the venue. Make sure there are no tables, buffet lines or other obstacles in the way of the paths you want people to follow, and be sure to have locations and the paths for getting there clearly marked with signs and such. Also, be sure to build enough time into the event schedule to allow for people to move from one place to another; a large crowd will move more slowly, for example, than a medium or small crowd.

- **Is your event an awards dinner ceremony?** If so, and if you are planning to start the awards after dinner, then calculate how long it will take to serve and eat dinner, clear away plates, begin the award ceremony, and present the awards to all of the recipients. In general, you're not going to get the group to stick around much longer than 60 to 90 minutes for the awards themselves, so plan the timing of dinner and the ceremony accordingly. Arrange for sufficient audio-visual equipment, as well as lighting and any other specialty equipment necessary for the awards show. Also, if recipients will be coming up to the stage to receive their awards, arrange the room to make it easy for them to move up and back, and build in enough time to the awards ceremony to account for any speeches or thank you statements the recipients might want to make.

- **What kind of entertainment will you have and how long will each act last?** Some types of entertainment, such as comedy acts, magic acts and interactive activities, require the audience to sit and pay attention, which means they'll need to be short enough to keep the audience from getting bored or restless along the way. Other types of entertainment, such as instrumental music, DJs, and similar activities can take place more in the background while people are occupied with drinking, eating and chatting, so they can be a bit longer to fill up this more extended length of time.

- **Will speeches be given?** If so, then you'll need to arrange for a stage, lighting, microphones, a podium and perhaps other stage props. Make sure the room is set up so the audience can see and hear the speakers from any spot in the venue and, if the speakers will be coming up from the audience, allow an appropriate walkway and stairs up to the stage to make their movement easy and prompt. Also, find out in advance if any of the speakers will be using visual aids such as PowerPoint slides, charts or other items, and plan accordingly for their needs.

- **How will you deal with requests from speakers?** In most cases, the scheduled speakers will have one or more requests for various items and set-ups to make their speeches more comfortable for them. For instance, they might want access to a wireless microphone rather than a handheld microphone; or, they might want bottled water instead of a pitcher of water and a glass. Some speakers ask for podiums of a specific shape and height, while others don't want a podium at all and instead prefer to move around the stage with perhaps just a simple stool and tall table to hold their water or other beverage. Find out all these things well in advance so you can have everything they request ready to go at the event.

- **Will a video be presented?** If so, then you'll need to determine the format to be used (DVD, computer animation, PowerPoint presentation, etc.) and the correct equipment to accommodate that format. If the venue is large, you'll probably want at least one (or maybe more) large screens at the front of the room, as well as other smaller screens or closed circuit monitors located throughout the room to allow everyone in the audience to have a good view.

- **Will you have celebrities, official guests, security escorts, or the like?** It is common for these kinds of people to have special needs, including access to a separate entrance or exit, opportunities to meet and mingle with the guests, or perhaps a table set up for autographs, book signing, record signing, etc. Again, find out as much as you can about their requirements well in advance so you can be sure to have everything in place at the event. It may even be a good idea to rehearse things like entrances, exits, and any other special adaptations in advance, so that your staff is well prepared and knows what to expect.

- **Will you need a band for dancing music or use a DJ?** This decision will determine all kinds of equipment needs, from extra space, a stage and lighting for a live band, to a dance floor, electrical power, stereo equipment, fancy lights and a microphone for a DJ. Keep in mind that a band will require additional space away from the actual event venue for storing instrument cases, warming up prior to their performance and generally getting ready for their time on stage.

KEY FOR SUCCESS

Always be flexible when determining the starting and ending times, since these can always be changed during the production process. During the event itself, you can also change the timeline as activities warrant, so again, flexibility in your thinking is a very good thing.

The answers to all of these and similar questions will help you prepare your preliminary timeline. It is important to remember not to schedule activities too close together because you risk derailing your timeline due to unanticipated delays, for example, and you are at greater risk for making miscalculations.

Keep in mind, however, that the purpose of this book is to help you start and run your event planning home-based business; creating a good timeline is a much more detailed and laborious task than I have presented here and there is no way to cover it in its entirety within the limited space of this book. However, I've done my best to at least provide you with a good starting point from which to learn and move forward.

As I stated in a previous chapter, I don't want this book to be 1,000+ pages long because that would simply be too long, too complicated and too unwieldy to be of much use for you. If you want more information and a more detailed discussion on the topic of designing timelines, I would recommend you view some actual event timeline samples—I'll give you one in a little bit—and learn about more considerations to bear in mind when creating one by visiting my web site at www.JorgeZurita.com

For now, I just recommend that you stay very realistic regarding the timing and timeline of your events. Calculate time frames for activities realistically so that you can guarantee everything will be ready on time from start to finish without rushing, and without risking your guests lapsing into boredom because one activity takes too long.

Another very important thing to consider in your timeline is the use of the venue including loading-in and loading-out schedules. Nowadays, a special event can take place virtually anywhere: hotels, ballrooms, convention and exhibition centers, country clubs, gardens, museums, universities, art galleries, historic venues, public places, restaurants, nightclubs, public buildings, lofts, shopping malls, roof gardens, parking lots, parks and theme parks, warehouses, empty lots and many more such places are all quite possible and can be excellent choices for the right kind of event.

Depending on the selected venue, you must gather information to complete your schedules for access to the space that includes time set aside for load-in and tear-down, delivery, use of freight elevators and storage to name but a few. That way, you will have every possible piece of information to consider, such as when it's easiest and when it's most difficult to physically get to the event area for load-in, what you need to do to book use of the freight elevator, any limitations there might be on how and when you access the venue and surrounding areas, and just about everything else you need to know to make the entire event run smoothly from set up to tear down and everywhere in between.

It is also useful to determine ahead of time whether you will have to pay for loading-in earlier or tearing-down outside of the "allowed" time under the official venue policies and procedures. Find out if there are more events taking place in the same venue, or if there are more vendors besides yourself coming in for the same event. Multiple events or vendors will result in overuse or over-demand of the same entrances, and the allotted time and services that the venue provides to suppliers will thus be quite tight. So, don't get caught by surprise; always be informed and keep yourself one step ahead of everybody else so you won't negatively affect the flow of your event. In the end, it will help you have a much more organized and successful event.

I also strongly suggest that you create an event folder or binder; I call mine the "Event Master File". You can use this tool to pull together all of the information relevant to your event such as your timeline, contracts, layouts, floor plans, seating plans, guest lists, relevant e-mail correspondence, contact information for all parties involved, invoices, contingency plan, estimates, menus, notes, miscellaneous items and any other information you can keep track of that can be useful for better organization and coordination of the event from start to finish and even afterwards.

It is also a great source of reference for future events, both with repeat and with new clients. Of course, not all events include all the items or documents from the sections listed above, so don't be afraid to customize your event folder or binder based on your unique needs. Depending on the event, you can always add or subtract new or existing binder subcategories as necessary along the way.

BEFORE: A FEW DAYS PRIOR TO THE EVENT

Your event timeline should start from the point at which the contract is drafted and paid for (either with a down payment or payment in full) and continue all the way up to the actual date and completion of the event as each particular project requires.

I like to refer to putting on an event as "Show Time." I always tell my staff, "The Event is King" and they all know that the meaning of that simple and odd phrase is that everything we do day-in and day-out, all of our efforts, start to make sense and take shape through making THE EVENT a reality.

The Event is King because the event itself is the reason we are in business in the first place. It is the embodiment of all of our company efforts, and this idea drives our philosophy and total commitment to excellence in everything we do. This idea also helps guide everything we do at all levels within our business, even when it involves making a difficult decision.

In my business, when we face a dilemma regarding the way we manage our business and projects, we always remind ourselves that "The Event is King." That way, if a certain action favors the successful outcome of our event production activities, or of any particular and actual event, we definitely go for it.

Keeping in mind the concept that "The Event is King," our performance during the planning stages is most important to an event's ultimately successful outcome. As I said, running the event itself means "Show Time" and everybody on board should give and do their very best to create a truly memorable experience for our guests and also keep every one of our valued clients happy.

As I said before, during the days just before the event there are certain crucial tasks you have to take into consideration. Here are the ones I consider most important. Your list may be longer or shorter, but inevitably you will have to deal with these issues a few days before the event actually happens:

Make sure your load-in and load-out schedules are sent/transmitted to and confirmed by all necessary vendors, including your own people, as well as to the venue. This will assure everyone is coordinated and ready on the day of the event.

Make sure that all stakeholders such as vendors and staff understand everything on their schedules, including every action they are expected to take or every service they are supposed to provide.

Review details of the event with your photographer and videographer so that they know what the event is going to be about. This allows them to establish which aspects of it they should pay more attention to vis-à-vis recording or photographing the event activities.

Confirm the final number of guests and get the final number to the caterer.

Follow up with every single vendor and briefly review the general terms of their particular contracts to refresh their understanding of their obligations.

DURING: THE DAY OF THE EVENT

On the day of the event, make sure you arrive before all of your vendors. You also want to make sure all your staff members arrive on site on time and with all the necessary documentation and/or an event file in hand, ready to start. Also, touch base with your venue contact as soon as you arrive.

Hold a brief meeting with your key staff to quickly review every point on the event itinerary. You want to make sure nothing is missing and that everyone understands what he or she is supposed to do at every point in the event process.

It is often necessary to conduct rehearsals, especially when there are speeches, presentations, performances or when the MC (master of ceremonies) is delivering messages the client wants to communicate, among other things. Remember, coordination and order are the key factors in making sure these rehearsals are smooth and successful. I always encourage my staff to arrange rehearsals right before the event starts, just to make sure all of the kinks are worked out. This might seem like a minor detail, but believe me it makes a huge, huge difference. There is a world of difference between the quality of a rehearsed event act and an improvised one. They say practice makes perfect, and in the case of event performance this is absolutely true.

At least one hour before the event starts, everything (and I mean absolutely 100% of the set-up) should be complete. At least 30 minutes before the guests arrive, all services and the corresponding personnel and staff should be in place; this includes bartenders, waiters, valet, photographer, videographer, MC, coordinators, talent, music, and cloak room attendants.

Make sure you have contact information for all of your vendors, your talent or the talent agency, and call them the minute after they are supposed to arrive to find out where they are. This will allow you to make better decisions in case somebody is delayed.

Additionally, bring the following documents from your event file:

- Contact sheet

- Load-in and load-out schedule

- Event timeline

- Floor plan

- Menu

Make sure every member of your staff has a copy of each of these documents as well. Each vendor should be provided with your contact information, his own particular load-in/load-out schedule and the event timeline.

REMEMBER...

Once the event starts, it is the equivalent of opening the curtain in a theater play.

As I stated earlier, the event means "Show Time." Your guests' experience begins the moment they enter the venue. Sometimes you'll use registration, so make visible signs and put them up high so guests can see them from a line. Have special greeters receive the VIPs so they can avoid the check-in process.

If you are using credentials, try to pick appropriate ones for the occasion and make sure they are visible and not easy to duplicate. You can use badges, pins, or wristbands; or, for more elegant events, you can use the invitation itself, or even a giveaway for theme events. For example, you can have a hat as credential and giveaway at a cowboy theme party. Use credentials also for your staff and vendors; try to be creative and have fun when designing them; it adds to the fun and enjoyment of the event for everyone involved.

If possible, put one person in charge of each one or two of the main services: one each for valet, registration, catering, audio/visual, entertainment, security, media team and ambulance (for crowded events). Establish a chain of command and communicate it to your staff and the venue's contact as well. Also, clearly establish who the decision makers are; if you don't do this I promise you will hear arguments about silly things like, "Who changed the location of the stage?" or, "Who authorized this or that charge?" This kind of situation will make you lose control of things really quickly, plus it looks really unprofessional. Finally, it is ok to say, "No," to last minute requests; just do it in a way that they understand the reason why.

Just remember that an event runs flawlessly (or not) depending on how well you coordinate the efforts of all your vendors, the venue, the staff and, of course, your client. In other words, event success depends on how well your operations are conducted.

FACT:

One of the absolutely key elements of a successful event (apart from a complete, well–structured, organized event kit) is the quality and completeness of communication between each and every vendor and members of your staff.

We've talked about communication before, and when it comes to execution of the event itself this is even more vital and crucial to success. That communication should flow through you at all times so you are always informed of everything that is going on during the event. At my events, the event team always uses radios to stay in communication with key people involved in event operations; this allows us to stay up to date on multiple activities and allows us to be in many places at the same time.

A timeline is always specific and varies depending on the type of event you are organizing; in fact, there is actually no single way to do it that applies all of the time and in all situations. A corporate event timeline, for instance, will be different from a wedding event timeline.

For the sake of example, on the next page you will find a sample version of a Brazilian-themed corporate event timeline.

BRAZILIAN THEMED CORPORATE EVENT TIMELINE

7:45 PM   Everybody in place

8:00 PM   Guests begin to arrive/greeted by stilt walkers

Bar opens and caipirina drinks are offered

Background samba singer performs w/ live band (Foyer)

8:45 PM   CD music in ballroom (bossa nova)

Ballroom doors open

Guests enter ballroom and sit

9:00 PM   First course is served at the tables

Intermezzo is served

Entrée is served

9:45 PM   Dessert and coffee are served

9: 50 PM   MC introduces the Capoeristas

10:00 PM   Batucada Parade (unannounced)

Dancers/animators invite guests to join pa-rade (dance floor)

10:25 PM   Live samba band in place ready to start (stage)

10:30 PM   Samba band takes over and plays dancing music

12:00 PM   Event ends

You can include many other things in an event like this, such as video projection, speeches and awards. You have to place each and every one of these items on the schedule in a way that helps the event flow naturally, but without cramming too many things into too short a time span.

Be aware that events are almost like a living creature; they move, change and transform over time. As an event planner, you are in charge and as such you are also as responsible for a job well done as you are for problems and last-minute issues. Along the way you will encounter difficult (cranky) guests, delayed vendors, audio visual equipment that fails, cold food, hot ballrooms, noise from another event in the same venue, lost items and other unexpected annoyances. If it can go wrong or cause a problem, believe me, it will, so please BE PREPARED.

The key to success is to always do the best that you can, use your best judgment, always look calm, remain in control, and keep your composure at all times. If you can master this then you can master any event!

AFTER: FOLLOWING COMPLETION OF THE EVENT

After the event is over, you may feel like you need to rest. You probably haven't even eaten and you're bound to feel really tired; however, nothing but nothing compares to the satisfaction that a successful and well-orchestrated event gives you. It's okay to enjoy this feeling, but just for a brief moment because remember... you are still not done with any particular event until you do a few more things.

The first action is to review whether any extra charges need to be assessed. You do this by asking any of your decision makers if they authorized any charges, let's say for an extra hour of alcoholic beverage service because your party ran on longer than expected, or paying the jazz band for another set of music.

If your event had any overages, you will have to deal with them and pay them as well, plus pay any of the vendors to whom you may still owe money. Don't wait until later to settle these issues, take care of them right then and there. If you expect your vendor to contact you to charge for the extras or you let much time go, either you or your vendor could forget the details regarding the extra charges and end up having difficulty deciphering what is actually owed.

The second thing you need to do is send your client an evaluation form from which you can determine their level of satisfaction. You want to ask your client questions such as:

- Was everything on time?

- How was the entertainment?

- How was the food?

- Was the event complete to your expectations?

- How were the decorations?

- How would you rate the services overall?

These are just a very few sample questions. For your own needs, you will want to prepare a more comprehensive evaluation form so you can gain valuable feedback about your service.

What is the best way to provide this evaluation form to the client? You can send it via e-mail and have it returned the same way, you can hand deliver it at the end of the event or you can mail it or fax it. It's a good idea to ask the client in advance how they wish to receive the evaluation form so you can provide it to them in the way that's most convenient and useful for them.

Be prepared for your client to point out things that went wrong or needed improvement, as well as things that went right and were completely satisfactory. This is to be expected and welcomed because it is the kind of honest feedback that is most useful to you and your team.

When the feedback comes in, be sure to let your team know about it, both the good and the not-so-good. Remember, by communicating this valuable information to everyone involved in the event, they can all participate in finding solutions to any problems identified or aspects of the event that could have been done better. Perhaps even more importantly, it also offers motivation to achieve excellence on future jobs and opportunities to give praise for a job well done.

Finally, it is highly recommended that you send a brief but professional "Thank You" note to your client, as well as to your vendors, especially those who did an outstanding job. This small personal touch helps you build a positive, long and promising business relationship with all of these people, adding greatly to the likelihood of earning repeat business and future referrals.

Some people say it is acceptable to send these thank you notes via email, but I much prefer (and my clients and vendors seem to prefer) sending them via regular mail and with your personal signature on the bottom of the card. This not only shows your appreciation, but also shows you respect and value them enough to take the time necessary to personally take care of thanking them for their efforts and business.

Never lose sight of the fact that events happen thanks to a team effort. The best and most successful endeavors only come about thanks to the efforts and enthusiasm of the best teams, highly skilled groups of people whose professionalism and coordinated actions are grounded in mutual respect for all parties involved.

Getting a deeper understanding on this matter will help you a lot in all your future events. To stay up to date and learn my latest secrets on this topic, join my insiders list for free at www.MasteringEventPlanning.com

CHAPTER RECAP

1. Event prep, planning, and execution are vital to a successful outcome. Follow the activities and steps discussed in detail in this chapter to be successful with your events, no matter the size, location, or occasion.

2. Pre-event planning involves spending time gathering crucial information necessary to begin and complete the production process. This information includes:

- Where will the event take place?
- What kind of event will it be?
- Who is the event for, how many and what kind of attendees will be there?
- When will the event take place?
- What is the client's real, actual budget?
- Will guests attend with their families?
- Will the guests be men, women or an even balance of the two?
- How many guests will attend?
- Are the guests primarily couples or singles?
- What is the average age of the guests?
- Do the guests know each other?
- Are the guests local or from out of town?
- Do the guests work for the same company?
- What else can you do to profile and understand the guests?

3. Put a contract in place that specifies and covers all of the details and specifics of the event. Have the contract prepared and ready to go so that you and the client agree on the scope of the project, each party's obligations, and so that both of you are protected from liability. Create a basic contract format that you can use as a template for a variety of situations and applications. At minimum, the contract should include:

- What services are included, when, where and at what time
- Price and payment terms
- Number of people included as staff
- Schedule for loading in/loading out

- Amount of time needed for set-up
- Your specific requirements to provide the services
- Any extra charges that may apply
- Cancellation policies

4. Review the contract terms carefully to determine all of your obligations, including if you can manage the event yourself or if you will need to bring in help. Use the contract to help you create a detailed, specific timeline for the event. The timeline may change as you move through the planning process, but that is to be expected; it is critical to have one though, because it dictates everything you do and negotiate along the way.

5. When creating a timeline, consider questions such as:
- On what day of the week will the event happen?
- What are you serving at the event?
- Will the guests move about during the event?
- Is the event an awards dinner ceremony?
- What kinds of entertainment will there be and how long will each act last?
- Will speeches be given?
- How will you deal with requests from speakers?
- Will a video be presented?
- Will you have celebrities, official guests, security escorts or the like?
- Will you need a band for music or use a DJ?

The answers to these and similar questions will help a great deal in preparing your preliminary timeline.

6. Putting on the event is "Show Time" and "The Event is King." This is the kind of attitude that's necessary to create the best, most memorable, most fantastic event possible.

Remember, the event is the reason you are in business in the first place. It is the idea that drives everything you do and your total commitment to excellence.

7. A few days prior to the event, review the crucial tasks and deliverables for the event, such as:

- Send/transmit load-in and load-out schedules to all parties, including vendors, suppliers and your own people
- Make sure every stakeholder understands everything on his/her schedule
- Review details of the event with the photographer and/or videographer
- Confirm the final number of guests and get that number to the caterer
- Follow up with each vendor, reviewing and confirming their contracts and obligations

8. On the day of the event, everything must come together as planned and it is your job to oversee the entire process. Establish contact with your venue contact and hold a brief meeting with your staff to quickly review the event itinerary. Ensure all set-up is complete at least 1 hour prior to the event, and all services and personnel are ready to go at least 30 minutes prior to guests beginning to arrive. Also, bring along all key documents, contact sheets, timeline, floor plan, and the menu.

9. After the event is finished, you still have plenty of tasks and responsibilities to take care of, such as:

- Reviewing if any extra charges are needed
- Taking care of any overages
- Sending your client an evaluation form to determine their level of satisfaction with each aspect of the event

Remember, the success or failure of an event is based not on your opinion about how things went, but rather on the client's opinion about how things went. When the client's feedback comes in, be sure to share it with your staff, giving recognition and praise when appropriate and constructive feedback when appropriate as well.

CHAPTER 10

WORKING WITH VENDORS AND NEGOTIATING DEALS

"Make every bargain clear and plain, that none may afterwards complain."

- Greek Proverb

THE KEY FACTORS TO CONSIDER

When organizing an event, you will need to identify different types of services depending on the specific type of event you are organizing, so knowing where to find the best and most reliable vendors for each service, and understanding how to negotiate the best deal for that service, become crucial tasks in your event planning career. You also need to understand which matters are or are not negotiable as well as issues related to make sure you get everything covered for your event.

In negotiating a contract with a vendor, therefore, it is very important to know how to:

- Get the best deal

- Protect your company

- Protect your client and the event itself

- Work within your budget so you turn a profit

- Pay attention to the most frequently overlooked issues during negotiation

When a client buys anything, he or she is always seeking the best possible deal and the exact same principle applies in the event planning industry. There are a wide variety of services and infinite potential vendors of the same service, so to cover all possible negotiation techniques would be next to impossible. Nevertheless, I will discuss some of the negotiation techniques that I use when hiring a vendor for an event and that have worked well for me.

WORKING WITH VENDORS AND THEIR SERVICES

In Chapter 2 I listed some of the most common services you can use when organizing an event, such as:

- Catering

- Venues

- Web programmers

- Rentals

- Floral arrangements

- Tents, stages and dance floors

- Audiovisual equipment for presentations

- Lighting

- Photographer

- Videographer

- Ice sculptures

- Wedding cakes

- Sound equipment

- Dee-Jay Bands and musicians

- Models and hostesses

- Talent agency

- Party favors

- Bathroom trailers

- MCs and animators

- Special effects/pyrotechnics

- Linens

- Rentals

- Furniture

- Themed décor

- Live entertainers

- Staffing

- Security

- Registry control

- Costumes

- Decorative fabrics

- Language interpreters

- Valet parking

- Graphic design

- Printing

- Games and inflatables

- Insurance brokers

- Speakers

- Promotional gifts companies

More often than not, locating these types of vendors is actually quite easy; what is challenging, however, is finding a professional and reliable vendor who can meet both your needs and budget for a particular event.

FACT:

The most common way to find vendors (apart from referrals from colleagues, family, and friends) is through the Internet, so I always begin there.

Once you have identified a few possible choices, you have to do some additional homework to make sure they can deliver their services as represented in their website, and further, deliver those services in a manner that suits your particular needs.

As the potential "employer," the burden then falls on you to follow up with appropriate inquiries. You must not only request their credentials, but also their portfolio and, most importantly, references from previous clients to contact and inquire about this particular vendor. Then, you must take it to the next level by conducting a personal interview with the vendor regarding their expertise, any insight they may have into your particular event type and any suggestions they may have to make your event more successful.

And these are just a few sample topics to include in the interview; as you become more experienced at the process of interviewing people, you will develop your own questions and "formula" for ensuring you hire the right person for the job.

Some essential questions I always ask are "How long have you been in business?" and "What other events have you worked and for whom?" Following this, I try to locate a person from the industry whom we both know so I can ask this objective third person for an opinion about the vendor. I would also suggest that you visit the vendor's website and ask your venue contact if he/she knows the vendor, which leads me to the next point.

I also make a point of calling this contact's venue directly before seeking alternatives. This saves you tons of time when that contact can offer suggestions, but with one caveat: This only applies if the service I'm seeking is not one the venue is also interested in providing either directly or through one of their own third-party vendors. It is a fine line to choose the right questions to get the information you need, while avoiding any conflict with the venue, when both, you and them, are trying to sell the same service to the same customer.

I would also recommend you issue an ITQ (Invitation to Quote) from multiple vendors of the same service. In the ITQ process, each vendor submits a bid that shows the scope of their service(s) and a price. This gives you a choice from a pool of vendors which, in turn, makes it easier for you to hire for each respective event. Make sure to provide all of the detailed information they need to prepare a thorough quote/bid, and that everything from their information to the quote itself is done in writing.

Take into consideration that more and more venues, especially hotels with convention centers and event facilities, are interested in providing other services through third-party suppliers rather than simply offering traditional event space, food and beverages. They can offer clients everything from floral arrangements, live entertainment and talent, and special décor to games and activities. Why do they choose to do this? It's simple, really; they want to expand their business and increase their revenues.

FACT:

It is always good business practice to do your own research to ensure you're making the best decision based on your specific needs and budget.

When hotels and convention centers already have an in-house or preferred vendor, it is a fair bet that these companies are indeed professional and reliable. But keep in mind that when you hire these in-house companies you should be prepared to pay a higher price than on the open market for the same type of vendors, since the in-house companies pay a commission to the venue for the referral. However, this is not set in stone and your situation can vary from event to event.

Also, be aware that some hotels with convention facilities will charge a fee for <u>not</u> using their in-house company. They will tell you that they have an "exclusivity clause" with them, so they need to charge you a certain amount of money as either a penalty or compensation for the refusal of their vendors. This is why it is so important to understand the rules; clearly identify your goals and objectives and those of the event, do your math and make sure you don't create a conflict with the venue, an in-house company and especially with your client when hiring a vendor for your event.

Prioritize your needs and then decide what you want and in what order. But above all, make sure you take the steps to hire a professional and reliable vendor who guarantees his delivery of services and thereby helps achieve a successful event.

It is always good for me to tell my "war stories" to emphasize a point, so here's a good example to consider. Let's say you already have some quotations in your hands and have reviewed them thoroughly. Select your finalists for every different service you will be providing at your event; these finalists should be the vendors who, at first blush, appear to meet your needs to a tee. I learned the hard way that you still are not done with the preliminary work before you even make the first verbal contact with the vendors on your list.

You also have to review all resumes, or whatever documents you have accepted as a basis to make your choice. If for any reason, your vendor quotation is missing an important piece of information, do not be shy or hesitate to go back to them and request that information. Also, be prepared for some of the vendors not selected to ask why you did not select them. Here it is important for you to understand this is not personal, it's business.

Leave your emotions at the door because the professional criticism will help them land another job, maybe even with you, if they correct what you perceived as a shortcoming. It is always the best practice to tell them your reasons in an upfront and educated way. You can always explain your decision-making process and lay out the most important factors that influenced your decision.

NEGOTIATING THE BEST DEALS

There is a very famous book on negotiation entitled "Getting to Yes: Negotiating Agreement Without Giving In"

(Roger Fisher, William L. Ury, and Bruce Patton). To negotiate effectively, you should understand the basic principles of the negotiation process and master some simple yet effective negotiation techniques.

As you will discover in "Getting to Yes," there are different styles of negotiation, the two primary ones being collaborative and competitive. As the names suggest, collaborative situations result in a "win-win" scenario whereas competitive negotiation results in a "win-lose" scenario.

Some of the diferentes between Competitive and Collaborative negotiations are summarized in the following table:

Characteristic	Competitive approach	Collaborative approach
Relationship	Temporary	Long-term
Consideration	Self	Both parties
Atmosphere	Distrust	Trust
Focus	Positions	Interest
Aim to gain	Advantage, concession	Fair agreement
Information	Concealed, power	Shared, open
Strategy	End justifies means	Objective and fair rules
Tactics	Coercion, tricks	Stick to principles
Outcome	Win-lose	Win-win

There is also the negotiation style that is "balanced" insofar as you use techniques from both the competitive and collaborative styles. In the event planning business, when dealing with vendors and hiring the venue, I would strongly urge you to follow a balanced negotiation style and close good deals for both parties.

The starting point of any negotiation is to know the following key points:

- What does the vendor want?

- What do you want?

- What is the price of the service in the open market?

- Who is the decision maker so you can try to deal only with him/her?

- What is your second most acceptable option?

- What points might create an impasse so you have to take a break?

- Which of your terms are negotiable?

- Which of your terms are non-negotiable?

- What are you willing to concede?

- What is your breaking point (the point when you say, "No")?

- What other critical factors or information relate to the negotiation?

- How can you best use your leverage?

In other words, never enter a negotiation blind, or you will end up being blindsided and paying too much. It might help to make a list of these points and any other relevant aspects to take to your event negotiation process in order to help you make a better decision and still get to yes.

There are also some points which are unique to the special event planning business, but which are often overlooked. I am sure you have already figured out that there are many factors involved in a business deal which involves hiring vendors for your event, aside from price, time and quantity. These factors may or may not apply depending on the type of service and vendor you are dealing with.

But because they offer alternative possibilities when negotiating and closing a deal, you have to make darn sure to address these issues when applicable in your contracts and in writing. If you ignore or overlook them, you will run into unwelcome surprises for you, your staff and your clients. By contrast, if you take these factors into consideration, not only do you look professional and avoid unwanted surprises and annoyances, but you can use these factors to negotiate better deals too.

For example, the following items are ones that you usually have to pay for, and oftentimes you can utilize them when negotiating with the venue

- Equipment setup

- Electricity and air conditioning, especially while setting up the equipment and/or during night shifts.

- Service charges and gratuities

- Cleaning fees

- Loading dock access

- Labor to change room settings

- Internet access

- Parking

- Security

- Cloakroom

- Extra hours at the venue or AV equipment when the event lasts longer than anticipated

- Service elevator

- Technicians

- Staging

- Risers

- Music licensing and/or union permits

- Venue permits if the event is held in a public place

As should be obvious from the length of this list, you can potentially use any of these factors to better negotiate outside straight price or quantity to organize a better and more professional event and obtain a better overall deal for the event.

KEY TO SUCCESS

Be creative, do reasonable tradeoffs and please, always try to get into a win-win situation so the final outcome of the negotiation benefits both parties involved. Never put the event or its quality at risk by taking a win-lose approach to negotiations.

Have you ever heard the phrase, "In business you don't get what you deserve, but what you negotiate?" In my opinion, that's absolutely true for the event planning business.

Just remember this: you negotiate every day and a quality negotiation should be based on a "win-win" principle. So, don't take advantage of other people; be intelligent with your money and get better deals by playing with all the resources and factors that I have mentioned or that are already at your disposal. Also, there are cardinal rules that you should always abide by. For example, always respect your counterpart and never misrepresent yourself just to get a better deal. Never, under any circumstances, coordinate a deal which puts the other party at an unfair advantage. Remember that when a deal is good for both parties, this will lead to more productive and positive deals down the line. When you can build strong and long-lasting relationships with vendors and suppliers, you will save time and money negotiating in the future.

A MUST DO LIST FOR SUCCESSFUL NEGOTIATIONS

With over 20 years of professional event planning experience, I have been involved in literally thousands of negotiations, so naturally I have learned a few tips and tricks along the way. Based on this experience, I have put together this "must do" list for engaging in successful negotiations.

1. ASK – YOU GET WHAT YOU ASK FOR

A better way to put this would be "You will never get what you want if you don't ask for it." How will a vendor ever know your expectations if you don't ask? It can be as simple as "Can you include in your price a simple dessert for 500 people? After all, we are bringing a big group and are getting you all this and that." If you don't ask this question, you will not have the opportunity to save money which could be used as part of your budget or, for example, to buy prizes.

2. CREATE AFFINITY/COMMONALITY

Just because you are negotiating does not mean you cannot find common, neutral and friendly ground. It can be as obvious as coming from the same professional background and knowing the same people, to having worked in the event planning business for many, many years. When you establish this kind of affinity/commonality, you will reduce the tendency of both parties to remain on the defensive when negotiating and make the overall negotiating process smoother and more effective. Remember, when someone feels comfortable with you personally, they can be more truthful about what is discussed. If you like someone, why not go ahead and tell that person that you feel that way?   When you can create a natural rapport with others it can go a long way towards improving your working relationship. These types of positive business relationships can last for many years to come.

3. SUGGEST COST EXPENSES IN A VOLUME NEGOTIATION

Let's say that you are purchasing drink cups, party favors, napkins, party streamers and the like (all items that would logically be sold by the case or lot rather than per piece), or you are hosting a huge event with lots of attendees and your vendor sells, say, bottled drinks. In this case, it makes sense to your bottom line to ask your vendor to sell you these types of items at a lower price in exchange for buying a considerable amount of cases in subsequent events or even right away. You will receive the savings and he/she will make more than the item's cost either way. But remember always hold true to your word and don't make these promises unless you honestly can make a volume purchase.

4. WHAT IF I PAY YOU CASH?

These are golden words to a vendor because it means they do not have to wait for a check to clear or pay the fee for a credit transaction (which can be as high as 4% to 5% in some cases). A cash transaction means they profit immediately, so if you make an offer to pay cash, they might cut you a deal and give you a discount. This reiterates the first principle: ASK.

5. HOW MUCH WOULD YOU TAKE OFF IF I PICK IT UP?

Most vendors charge a fee for delivery that is built into their overall price for things such as beverages, party goods, equipment (tables, chairs, etc.) and the like. If you have a reliable delivery service already under contract or can even take care of this yourself, it presents a good way to ask for and potentially get a discount.

6. WHEN IS THIS ITEM ON SALE?

Some items you need for certain events, say for a summer party, will go on sale at certain times during the year. It will not offend a vendor to ask when the items will be on sale. If their response is that it will be in two weeks' time or some other shorter period, it is ok for you to ask, "Can I have the sale price right now?" This allows the vendor the opportunity to make a sale which he might not otherwise have made.

7. DON'T GO FIRST; LET YOUR COUNTERPART SET HIS POSITION

A cardinal principle of good negotiation is never to volley the first shot. Ask the vendor, "What would you consider a fair price?" and let him or her throw out a figure. Then you can negotiate down from that point unless the first offer is so reasonable you would be a fool to pass it up.

8. NEVER NEGOTIATE AGAINST YOURSELF

This point begs the obvious. No vendor's products or services are so valuable that you should ever preface a negotiation volley with, "I'd pay twice as much if you... " and fill in the blank. You would be shooting yourself in the foot and the vendor will see you as an easy mark. Remember, "win-win" does not mean caving in to the vendor's every demand or selling yourself short to make a deal. Remember also that there is always someone else who can offer a better price if negotiations fail on the first run with the first vendor.

9. USE WEAKNESS AS A STRENGTH

In reality, this is your way of showing the vendor that you really need his or her particular services or goods. The approach is simple- after presenting what you need, say something like, "Help me, you're the only person who sells this around here," or, "I need you to help me out because I am just starting out and could really use a deal here. Everyone else knows this and tries to take advantage of me." Vendors will usually help someone just starting out and you can actually get a decent discount, again, provided that what you honestly portray your weaknesses. Obviously, if you have been in business a long time, it would be highly unscrupulous to use this strategy! Be sure to remain honest in all negotiations.

10. THIRD PARTY AUTHORITY

If you are working with another person, you can inspire a discount offer by saying, "Let me check that with my boss." These words will motivate vendors to reduce their prices for a quicker sale.

11. WHEN BUYING A PRODUCT OR SERVICE, SEND A FRONT PERSON TO START NEGOTIATIONS. THEN, AFTER NEGOTIATIONS ARE COMPLETE, WAIT A LITTLE TIME BEFORE COMING IN TO CLOSE THE DEAL AT A BETTER PRICE

No one wants to waste all the time invested in a sales lead, so a front person will save you valuable time and money since the vendor either is or is not going to offer a lower price.

12. PROTECT YOUR POSITION WITH THE "BLUE CHIPS-BARGAINING CHIPS" STRATEGY

Blue Chips: You've got to have them. Bargaining chips: it's nice to have them, but they're not necessary. Blue chips might be something like a DJ for a wedding, whereas a bargaining chip might be one certain type of sound equipment over another. One you have to have, while the other is more optional (and therefore negotiable) in nature.

13. NO ONE WANTS TO NEGOTIATE WITH SOMEONE WHO IS NOT WILLING TO GIVE IN A LITTLE

Sometimes it is good to pay a bit more than what we have planned, or give in a bit on some aspect, in order to come to an agreement that will be convenient for both parties. So, many times, you also have to be willing to give in your position or pay a bit more if you want to get a good deal for both you and the other party.

14. CREATE A COOPERATIVE ENVIRONMENT

Sit close to the other person at the table when negotiating. Claim that you have something to show the other party and when the time comes, comply. This creates a feeling of familiarity and respect, like you are doing business with a friend.

15. DON'T MAKE IT ANTAGONISTIC

You never want to bully someone into agreeing to your terms through threats or coercion. It will only serve to make them angry and damage your professional reputation. You can, however, politely yet firmly ask someone to be more reasonable in their terms if you feel they are somehow unreasonable or otherwise out of line. Remember that it is essential not to rip anyone off. But, by the same token, they should not rip you off either.

16. OPERATE ON YOUR HOME TURF

Having a potential vendor come to your home or your office location is making them come to you. It puts you in an inherent position of power and can open the door to better success at negotiating terms and discounts.

17. USE THE POWER OF PRINT: EVERY AGREEMENT IS "THE STANDARD FORM"

People are inherently suspicious of contracts, so you can allay those suspicions somewhat by offering the security of saying, "Oh, don't worry, this is the standard form I use with all my vendors" when presenting your contract. This will put the vendor more at ease and open the door to more concessions. It sounds weird to read this on this page, but when you say it in a negotiation it really works. Reassuring that the contract is nothing more than the "standard form" makes it easier to get the other person to sign on the dotted line, simply because it's in writing. However, of course, remember to act with integrity. Don't make this promise to another person unless it is, in fact, true. In other words, don't tell someone that it is a standard contract and then try to sneak something different by him or her.

18. DON'T KILL THE OTHER PARTY'S EFFORTS IN SUCH A WAY THEY CAN'T DELIVER

I know "kill" is a strong word, but it is appropriate. This follows the cardinal rule: DON'T PUT THE EVENT AT RISK by failing to allow a vendor to do what he/she does best and charge a fair price for it. Remember, you may be putting on the event, but a professional band, for example, knows that to load-in and load-out will take at least two hours and 4 people. But if you want them to do that particular task in less than an hour, be willing to pay the price for bringing extra staff to carry out that job properly. I guarantee you will put at risk or even ruin that event because it will put them in a horrible mood and they won't play well, not to mention that they might finish installing their equipment late, which also affects the overall result of your professional work as an event planner.

19. WHEN ASKED ABOUT YOUR BUDGET SAY, "I STILL NOT HAVE THE FINAL NUMBERS"

In certain occasions or with certain services, you should never, ever disclose your budget to your provider or vendor, because if they know you have $1,000 for floral arrangements, they will simply ask for it as their default position. It is true that in Chapter 9 I have talked about the great importance of knowing our client's budget for the whole event before starting planning, and I said that it was nonsense that some clients simply resist divulging this information up front on the assumption that if they tell you the true amount then you are going to figure out a way to charge them everything they have set aside for the event. Now, it can seem a contradiction that what applies for our client does not apply for us when we play the role of the client when dealing with our providers. But the truth is that sometimes a particular situation is against your interests, and other times that same situation, when roles change, can benefit you. When you take the role of vendor of your event planning services, you have to understand that alternatives are almost infinite when you have to present a proposal to your client that fits his/her needs and expectations, and so you have to start from a global number/amount to avoid offering something that doesn't fit the client's budget. While when we deal with a provider (that will probably offer one or more specific services for the event; but not the whole event like often times we do) the alternatives that he/she can provide us are much more limited, and that is why he/she doesn't need to know which is our budget in order to be able to tell us the cost for his products or services. That is the reason why in this case I recommend you to ask the price for the products or services that you are seeking, instead of disclosing your budget, since, as I explained before, it is very common that if you say that you have $1,000 available, the provider will think that he must ask for at least $1,000 despite the fact that his/her regular price for the same service is just $800. Besides, when you are preparing a proposal with prices, you don't usually know the budget for each item, because as an event planner you will start from a global amount that your client will give you to cover the entire event, and as I said, you will have infinite options to offer to your client and a wide variety of services required to produce an event.

20. CONSIDER POINTING OUT ESPECIALLY ATTRACTIVE- AND SURPRISING-POINTS OF YOUR BUSINESS OFFER AS YOU BEGIN TO REACH AN AGREEMENT.

While it helps to begin with an interesting option, one last positive fact of what you can offer will certainly re-energize the conversation even as you wind up, and leave those who need more time with an uplifting picture.

21. RESPECT CULTURAL DIFFERENCES IN INTERNATIONAL NEGOTIATIONS

As you meet with clients and vendors from other parts of the world, take the time to research etiquette basics in their culture. But go beyond: This isn't simply a matter of learning whether a handshake is in order when you meet. Don't forget that negotiating works slightly differently from one area of the world to the next. Some clients and even vendors expect to see the whole picture first and then begin to focus on details. Others (most Western hemisphere cultures) want to hear details before having a look at the whole. Some might respond strongly to choices you offer; others might be very reserved, even if their reactions are privately drastically different than you interpret.

22. REMEMBER THAT NEGOTIATING IS NOT ARGUING

You may disagree, but beyond quickly noting that you have different views, you do not stand to benefit by arguing your point—no matter how sure you are that you are right. You may be knowledgeable and right, but you'll do yourself a favor by not saying so bluntly and instead providing more useful information. Negotiation may involve the back and forth of an argument, but a win for you is not proving that you are right and the vendor wrong; a win is being able to agree on a plan that will benefit the vendor and be convenient for you.

23. BE VERY, VERY, VERY NICE

So, as you can see, negotiating is actually an art. It is the art of learning how to give and take in any business deal. Without the ability to concede certain points while still generating a profit for yourself, you will not succeed, and to conduct successful negotiations for both you and your counterpart, you have to be very, very, very nice. It really is that simple.

Remember, your client is not the only person involved in making the event successful. Your vendors and suppliers are the critical elements without whom there usually cannot even be an event in the first place. As you gain experience, you will learn how to deal with vendors and suppliers in your own unique way and with your own personal flair, but in this section I have provided you with some basic stepping stones that will help you ford the creek successfully before you get to where you must cross the larger river.

You can find additional negotiation techniques in my report called "The Event Planner's guide to hearing yes in negotiation" – and you can get it 100% free by joining my insiders list at www.MasteringEventPlanning.com.

CHAPTER RECAP

1. Working with vendors and negotiating deals are at the very heart and soul of your successful event planning business. You will only make a profit and succeed in business if you do these things well.

2. When negotiating a contract with a vendor, you must know how to:

- Get the best deal

- Protect your company

- Protect your client and the event

- Work within the budget so you turn a profit

- Pay attention to issues that are frequently overlooked

- Seek to coordinate a win-win situation

3. Working with vendors and suppliers requires you to pay attention to detail and fulfill the role of "employer" to ensure they are all capable of providing what you require. Interview each one carefully and thoroughly, and always check credentials and references.

4. Negotiating the best deals is all about understanding the basic principles of the negotiation process and mastering some simple yet effective negotiation techniques. Take a balanced negotiating approach, using a combination of competitive and collaborative styles to ensure the most productive and successful negotiations. Always enter negotiations with as much information as possible to put yourself in the best negotiating position possible.

5. Review the "Must Do List" items for successful negotiations. These tips, suggestions, and techniques come from my 20+ years of experience in the event planning industry and are key things that can help you negotiate anything with anyone and be more successful at it. Remember, the vendors and suppliers you negotiate with are vital components to making every event a resounding success.

CHAPTER 11

SELLING YOUR EVENT PLANNING SERVICES

"If it doesn't sell, it isn't creative."

-- David Ogilvy, British advertising executive

Selling your services as an event planner is a crucial task, as is selling in any other profession or business. In fact, one could argue (as I have repeatedly done in this book) that selling is the most important task you do, especially in the beginning. If you are serious about succeeding as an event planning professional, you must actively and effectively sell your event planning services. In this chapter I'm going to talk about a different approach to selling your event service that will help you improve your performance in this area.

A NEW APPROACH TO SELLING

A quick distinction between marketing and sales

Before I begin talking about the topic of a new approach to the way you sell your event services, I'd like to make a distinction between *marketing* and *sales*. These two differ-ent terms often confuse people, so let's start with a definition:

A couple of definitions that don't sound very academic but are really practical, are:

Marketing This would be anything you do to get or keep a customer

Sales Sales are all about the personal contact to close a deal.

These are simple definitions that you can remember very easily. Oftentimes, people who focus on sales and marketing claim that they are good at that, because they know how to convince people to buy something. But in my opinion, that is not what marketing and sales are all about. Again, marketing is anything you do to get or keep a customer and sales are the personal contacts—but without twisting arms, a tactic we often associate with sales. It means carefully listening to each client so that you can address and solve the client's unique needs.

And this implies a new perspective on selling compared to our common, traditional view of selling. Likely you'll agree with me that the majority of people try to avoid selling alto-gether. They dislike that activity. Why? Because selling has a bad reputation. Very few people want to say, "I'm in sales," because sales people are sometimes thought of as disrepu-table. And with good reason. There are thousands of ex-amples of tricks and scams committed by sales people over the years, people who sold anything, from fake watches to treasure maps to magic formulas. And this is only one part of the problem. The other problem is that traditional sales training still focuses on teaching how to convince people to buy from you, how to talk to prospective or potential customers, and how to overcome objections in order to close the sale—*no matter what.*

Trainers use terms borrowed from the sport of wrestling. A *half nelson close* in wrestling means that the wrestler uses one arm of the other athlete to win. With the full nelson, the wrestler holds the opponent under both arms, a dangerous stance that could if the wrestler pushed down, wind up with the opponent suffering a broken neck.   On the other hand, the *half nelson close*, a "one armed hold" a salesman attempts, leaves a client with one arm free—to sign the contract.

So this is the traditional image of sales. Sales trainers also employ terms from judo, also, to remind their salespeople to use the clients' own motion against him or her.   But think about this. These tactics eventually annoy and even drive away potential clients. If you try to sell your event services without an eye on an ultimate win/win situation, well, that relationship will not benefit any of the parties, and it will not develop into an ongoing, profitable relationship.

HOW TO APPLY SALES AND MARKETING TO YOUR BUSINESS

All right, now having differentiated Marketing and Sales, let me very quickly explain how applying the two goals can turn into a crucial component not only for an event business but for every event.

The relevance comes when you understand this simple idea:

YOU HAVE TO CREATE SYSTEMS

When it comes to marketing and sales, you actually have to create two different systems for each of these, different from each other yet working together to increase your sales:

The first type of system you have to create is one that will regularly make sure you draw potential and targeted customers into your door (the marketing side). This means you have to create one or more processes that result in your phone ringing with people on the other side of the line asking to get an estimate, a quote for the cost of an event.

On the other hand, you also must build a second system: the one that leads to customers buying from you. Your sales system should be made up of the actions that give you personal contact with the customer, keep that customer happy, and ultimately, keep the customer buying repeatedly.

There are plenty of examples to follow while creating your own version of these two complementary types of systems. This works in the same way that attendance at a free seminar, one with a perceived (and real) high value, leads to your signing up for another one and then another. The company has given you the initial seminar free to get customers to the door.

At the first free seminar, you are very happy with the knowledge you are acquiring. Seminar leaders then seize the moment to offer you yet another seminar, complementary to the first, not free, but at an irresistible price. You buy the second seminar. Then when you attend the second seminar, they offer you a third one, and you are so happy with the results of the first two that you actually buy the third.

This is how your own Sales system should work: It keeps your new customers happy, but more importantly, keeps them buying from you.

And once you have them buying from you, you start up-selling, cross-selling and down-selling them, but that I'm going to cover more extensively later in this chapter

Repeated sales and referrals

All right, now that we have covered this important distinction, let's turn to building a marketing and sales strategy that is a long-term strategy for your new or existing event business.

If you are planning to stay around for a long time, don't forget that your big profits don't come from the first event you sell to customers. They come from the repeated sales and referrals you get from them.

I recommend that you adopt a completely new approach to sales instead of going for the traditional, high-pressure methods. Consider this activity as a way to help people, and to help them identify and solve all of their needs. Meeting these needs—designing, planning and producing their events—not only assures you of more sales and profits. It also assures that you will form more friendships along the way. When you sell, try to meet new people, and when you do, learn about their needs and the needs of the businesses they are in. You will get paid if you are providing the right solutions every time. Don't be pushy, and ask as many relevant questions as possible. Learn as much as you can in your areas of expertise, and then provide the smartest and most efficient alternatives to meet your clients' needs.

Overcome your fear of rejection

We know that another major reason for reluctance when it comes to sales is the common fear of rejection. When we were little kids, we heard many times from adults, "No, don't touch that." Maybe they wanted to protect us from getting injured or injuring something. But the word *no* still brings real pain to us. Even as adults, when we hear the word, we're likely to instantly feel bad. It's simply an automatic reaction.

We are conditioned to interpret a *no* as a negative response. And yet at times we avoid trying something worthwhile because of it. We may lose many opportunities available, and all because we're so afraid of getting rejected. It's as if we're the shy boy at the party afraid to ask a nice girl to dance because she might say no. She may—or he could guarantee that he stands on the sidelines all evening by not taking this risk.

The same applies to us when we avoid offering our services upon meeting a potential customer convinced that this person will have no interest in our business. We believe that the client might respond with disinterest in our business. The potential client, we're certain, will say the dreaded word *no*.

Well, of course it's true that most of us tend to fear rejection. But consider this. If you truly have a good product or you provide excellent services—services that represent a lot of value for your customer, and services that you strongly believe your customers can benefit from—then taking a risk in order to possibly gain a new customer is worth the challenge. Even if the potential for rejection looms.

Think about it. Even if they reject you the first time, you end up taking away something positive from this attempt.

This is because you will be building a relationship with the person. You would also be practicing and improving your sales approach, and at the end, you'll have more chances of getting to work with this particular customer. People tend to do business with someone they have had a previous contact with rather than with someone they have never met before. The more familiar with you and your business these people are, the safer they feel in engaging in business with you. So I would suggest that you keep trying to get those juicy contracts, over and over again until you have built a relationship and your customer feels ready, comfortable, and safe to go on and sign with you for that important event.

You know the saying, "If something is worth doing, it's worth doing it right," and if you are not willing to practice your sales approach and do it better every time, you're never going to get it right.

My philosophy of selling and marketing is that you should be trying to find people who you can help in the best possible way. Being an event professional is something you can do more often than you think, because customers are always in need of new alternatives at competitive prices and superb quality. If you are the best in what you do, your event services will help your clients present successful events. Therefore, as these events bring success to your clients, thanks to you as the responsible planner, the clients will only want to continue this successful partnership.

Consulting Selling

Even though this approach to selling is not the common type among sales people in general, it's been around for more than 30 years. It's called *consulting selling*. Actually, this has evolved into a more generic term meaning roughly "act like a consultant." So, let's say your customer has a problem and you are a sales person. You know you want to sell them the whole event, but if you analyze his or her problems and offer him or her the right solutions for him, you have presented yourself as much more professional. This is also more helpful to him or to her than if you had tried to sell them only what you have instead. So, if you are honest and good, your answer will not always be "buy my services."

Sometimes you will tell him that he doesn't need this or that particular service for his event, and you'll tell him that he needs something else instead, probably something you don't even cover, and that's acting as a true consultant. You don't push what you have, you only help them solve their particular need. So a good consultant who is a professional sales person does a "needs analysis," and then recommends helping people with his advice, probably starting with the things he doesn't do, which is actually a very good way to show people that he's not someone who pushes his services, but someone who puts his/her clients first by suggesting and delivering what his customers need.

When a particular service is something you don't do, don't know, or don't include as one of your services, be honest and let your customer know that this is not your prime area. If you know of a reliable vendor specializing in the service, by all means recommend him or her to do the job directly. But tell your customer that you can best help him or her in the areas in which you are an expert . This will create almost immediate rapport and will help you gain your customer's confidence.

You will be coming across as a consultant; in other words, you'll be perceived as someone who's not just pushing things, trying to get every dollar out of your customer's pocket. So in general, that is what we mean by consultative selling, a term that actually most people are not familiar with, even in the sales profession.

The 5 Components of Consulting Selling

1. Building a Relationship

As I mentioned earlier, most sales training is still done the old fashion way: You learn how to give a presentation, how to talk about your product, its features and benefits, and how to handle objections, trying to close the deal almost on the spot. So in this scenario, you're trained to expect objections. However, when you are acting as a consultant or a friend, you don't get objections. You discuss things trying to help people overcome their needs and challenges when planning and executing events. And remember: The most important thing about consulting selling is building a relationship with your prospect—but rather than as a sales rep, a helpful consultant and a friend.

Remember, not everyone will want to hire you when they first meet you. They will appreciate more information, and will want to get your newsletter, so you should start one if you want to present yourself as a consultant.

2. Needs analysis

The second thing you should be focusing on is the *needs analysis*, which we will talk about again. It's fairly common sense, but there are some technicalities to it to keep in mind. You have to analyze what issues they have, how they might be helped. Analyze their needs; review Chapter 9 and gather all questions you will want to ask your customers to properly assess their needs.

3. Know your customer's business and industry

The third component is understanding their industry, their lives, and their context.   When it's about event planning, the approach should be more personal. You want to understand people's businesses. For example, if you are organizing events for a major car maker, you better understand the car dealing and manufacturing business.

By understanding their industry and their business situations, you will talk in their language. You will know the right recommendations and event concepts, and you will be saving precious time for them while preparing the event. Not to mention that ultimately you will be in a much better and consistent position to guarantee your client's event success.

4. Ask the right questions

First of all, you have to remember that all people are different. So to get along with different people, you don't treat them all the same, you treat them differently. Thus the fourth element of *consulting selling* is asking the right questions instead of just talking all the time. Resist the urge to talk about your services and products or how wonderful your events are. Instead, listen carefully and ask smart questions.

You learn about people. You build a relationship with your prospective customer, and that's actually treating them differently than other customers. The most basic reason that people like you is when you reinforce their individuality at some level, and a very good way to do that is by knowing who they are and what they want by asking them questions.

This way, you'll end up knowing your customer on a more personal level and knowing their specific needs for a particular event, which means that you will provide the right solutions. Also, you will be building a stronger relationship where reciprocity between you and your customer can play an important part on the path to friendship.

5. Be Creative

The fifth component of consulting selling is to be creative, to bring creative ideas to the negotiation. If you are a sales person, you are selling event services to people to help them accomplish their business objectives, so you have to learn how to be creative. Exercise this skill on a regular basis. Again, try not to offer at first the standard fare, or what you have in your sample case, but instead, get to know your customer by building up a relationship with him or her. Find out that customer's needs are and come up with creative alternatives to address every issue in an innovative, professional, and personalized fashion. When you help people succeed, you will succeed too.

Acting as a consultant as opposed as a sales person, and exploring all the possibilities to solve a particular need to your customer when selling your event services, will almost instantly position you as an authority in your particular field and gain you your customer's trust.

By utilizing this approach to selling, you will become a more successful and respected event planner, because you will be building stronger relationships and therefore, closing better deals.

So in conclusion, if you adopt this new approach when putting in motion your sales efforts, you'll be setting yourself up for better results in these areas. You will not be utilizing the hardcore sale approach. Therefore, you must do everything in your power to serve and help people by providing the best alternatives for them. Rather than trying to close a deal every time you go out there, your goal will be to make a new friend and try to help him or her with your vast knowledge in regards to event planning. You'll end up building stronger relationships, and even if a prospect doesn't hire you the first time you offer your services, you'll end up in a much better position for the next time. Remember that people tend to buy from people that they have previously known. Consulting selling is a much better approach to sell event services, since you present yourself as an expert and a friend that people want to do business with.

PUT YOURSELF IN CONTACT WITH THE RIGHT PEOPLE AND DESIGN CUSTOMIZED SOLUTIONS

FACT:

If you want to sell your event planning services effectively, you have to put yourself in contact with the right people and bring the right product or service to the table at the right time.

When I sell an event, I always try to understand and listen thoroughly to what my prospective clients are looking for, and then I ask as many relevant questions as possible, either by phone, e-mail or in person. I strive to provide them with the terms and conditions they are most interested in, except for the payment conditions that I mentioned in Chapter

9. I then communicate these same terms and conditions to my vendors, the venue and my staff to assure the solutions my prospective clients are most interested in will become a reality. In other words, I always put myself in contact with the right people, in order to keep good and updated communications with those in charge of each part of the puzzle.

During this process, you gain credibility, build trust and provide the right answers and solutions that your clients or prospects are seeking.

On the other hand, you have to be able to provide as much value as possible in such a way that you maximize, not minimize, your profit margins.

AVOIDING THE MOST COMMON MISTAKES

Along the way though, I have made my fair share of mistakes. To help you avoid making these same ones, I have put together a list of the most common errors made by new event planning professionals. You can get my free report "23 Most Common Mistakes to Avoid When Selling Your Event Services" at www.MasteringEventPlanning.com

CHAPTER RECAP

1. It is absolutely crucial that you address both Marketing and Sales to sell your event planning services successfully; in fact, it is arguably the most important task of all when you stop to consider that your primary goal is to make money. You must establish separate systems for how you will mar-

ket—get the customer in the door—and how you will make sales—that personal contact that leads to the sale—for your event business.

2. An event planner must engage in Consulting Sales: This means you must act as a consultant, asking your client about his or her requirements and expectations, while at the same time advising, using your own expertise.

3. Put yourself in contact with the right people in order to be most successful at selling your services and making money. It starts with targeted branding, followed by proper positioning of yourself and your business and finishing up with carefully planned meetings and presentations. Your goal is to gain credibility, build trust and provide clients and prospects with the solutions they want and need.

4. Avoid the most common mistakes made by new event planning professionals.

CHAPTER 12

LEADS, PROPOSALS, AND FOLLOW THROUGH

"Never over-promise, but always over-deliver."

- Jorge Zurita's formula for success – Event producer, consultant, and speaker.

PLANNING IS CRITICAL

KEY TO SUCCESS

Planning the logistics of an event may appear difficult at first, but if you do it correctly, your job will become much easier. It is good to remember to be as detail-oriented as you can, since a large event really is the amalgamation of many, many details.

To plan successful events, you have to consider all the logistics that will take place behind the scenes and which are critical to preparation and execution. In other words, a successful event planner always *plans* for success. What this means is that if you develop a detailed and well-designed plan for the event, you are set for success, while failure to plan properly will set you up for failure.

The concept of planning goes back to the basics: sales. If you want to succeed in this or any other business, not only do you have to learn some basic sales techniques and strategies like those from Chapter 11 (and a lot more), but you also have to come to understand the sales process when you are following up on leads.

FOLLOWING UP ON LEADS

After selling and planning events for many years, I've found that following up on leads for event planning services is a long and sometimes difficult process. There are many things to consider before a customer decides to go ahead with an event and retain your services as his planner. It is this sometimes lengthy decision-making process on the client's part that dictates why selling our services oftentimes involves a significant amount of effort with multiple tasks to be performed professionally and diligently.

In this field, time is always of the essence.

If you truly want to sell your services and outdo your competition, not only do you have to understand the nuts and bolts of the follow-up process, you also must be able to submit winning proposals that reflect that you understand what your customer is seeking. That, in turn, means you need to lay out in easy-to-understand language and graphics your precise scope of services and how the event will appear when it happens.

By doing this, you minimize the possibility of unpleasant surprises, misunderstandings and flaws. In legal terms, you are seeking a meeting of the minds with your client. Without it, chaos will control the event and your client will not be inclined to either give your name as a referral or retain your services again.

Let's say you are selling your event services to the corporate events market, and a corporation you have been involved with (either you have done something for them in the past or you presented yourself and your services when the opportunity arose) has already decided to organize an event. The corporation has already determined its goals and objectives, so it issues a Request for Proposal (RFP) that serves as a public invitation to you and other event planners to submit their bids.

A bid in this business is your business proposal for the event that includes price, scope of services for that price and your credentials that they can evaluate.

PREPARING WINNING PROPOSALS

Requests for Proposals are usually released when the sponsor or client is planning a high-ticket item that is usually a large event. It contains what this company is looking for from an event planner or venue and asks for bids based on certain requirements and guidelines.

In some cases, a company will issue an Invitation to Quote (ITQ) rather than an RFP, which is a less formal process to follow but still requires you to pay attention to the details and prepare your proposal for that particular requirement according to the specifics in the ITQ. However, because most companies tend to offer RFPs rather than ITQs, we're going to focus on the former for the rest of this section.

A company issues RFPs for any number of reasons. Sometimes internal policies require them to issue RFP´s (or by law, particularly in the government sector). They also do it to compare prices and terms among different vendors. This is the reason the RFPs are very specific and clear regarding what they're seeking. That way the comparison between vendors submitting bids are apples with apples.

MY BEST ADVICE:

Bid smart and select carefully the RFPs that you want to submit.

Sometimes they ask for more proposals than they need or have time to review, with the intention of negotiating a better price with the supplier they intend to do business with. Obviously, that is a good thing if you are the chosen supplier; but not so good when you are not because it causes you to lose time, energy and money with no chances of winning the project. Again, no disrespect by saying this, but sometimes this is true.

The RFP/bidding process usually starts with the company contacting your business by e-mail or phone and requesting you to submit a proposal. Once you have prepared the bid proposal, I recommend using e-mail to submit it (unless you are required to do it in person or in a sealed envelope) because using this type of written communication leaves less room to omit important details and reduces the possibility of making mistakes and forgetting crucial things.

Additionally, all parties involved have a record of whatever is discussed or dealt with during this part of the process. A few companies have implemented web-based RFP forms for vendors to fill out. But more often than not, this form of RFP is limited and does not allow much freedom to submit very specific or extensive proposals. I recommend you control this process and use your own documents and graphics until you are sure you can use such web-based utilities without compromising your image and the quality of your information.

Even though good RFPs are as detailed as possible, you can still have some questions or doubts. So unless the proposal explicitly states that it is not permitted, after receiving an RFP it is an acceptable business practice to send e-mails or make a phone call to clarify certain points and ask relevant questions. You can even arrange a meeting with your contact to discuss the matter in greater detail and make sure that you are on the same wavelength.

This will not only increase your chances of submitting a proposal that addresses your prospective client's needs to the letter, it also gives your contact a sense or a feeling that (s)he is being taken care of. But before you even consider contacting the issuing company, check the RFP guidelines for whether this is appropriate and acceptable. After receiving the RFP and having an interview or conference call with your contact, you are in a better position to create a winning proposal.

Your bid proposal should be presented with as much, if not more, detail than the RFP. First, make sure your proposal includes the following elements and information that will usually be contained in the RFP:

1. All RFPs ask for vital stats on your company. Use your business stationary or include your digital logo if you are submitting your bid by mail. Include all of your contact information: address including street number, city and zip code; your phone number(s) (business and mobile); your fax number; your e-mail address; and your name and title.

2. It is very important to include the following information regarding the event:

   -- Name of the event or any type of reference to it
   -- Probable locations beginning with the "best" option
   -- The probable or preferred dates and times
   -- Presenting alternatives if this information is not definitive
   -- Budget (optional)

3. RFPs should address the goals and objectives of the event, the number and profile of potential attendees (including percentages of males and females), where they are coming from, average ages of attendees and their positions within the company businesses to which they belong.

4. Often the RFPs include the history of past events similar to the one they plan on organizing so bidders can have a clearer idea of the event overall.

5. Requirements for meeting room spaces. Here you need to know the exact physical dimensions of your locations, the size of the tables and chairs, serving tables, stages (if applicable), a podium and any other equipment space you might need if, for example, you have a band or play to present. You also want to include hotel room rates and sizes if the event space is a distance away from the company and will require guests to spend the night. Of course you have to make sure that hotel rooms are available as well.

6. Food and beverage requirements. This element is critical, especially when serving alcohol at an "open bar." One thing most clients never want to happen is to run short of their guests' favorite drinks. It is good to get two or three quotes from alcohol vendors as the cost of this particular product will vary wildly. This gives the client a choice and a visible method of seeing that you can get a good deal on alcohol.

7. Transportation requirements. If your clients' guests need to go to and from the corporate headquarters, you had better include a way to make that happen. Check with your local transportation company. Some companies specialize in event transportation.

So, let's say the venue is a local museum. Well, anyone who has ever parked way out in the parking lot knows that a walk to the entrance is not appreciated. Use a van or two from a transportation service provider to make that commute easier. You also want to include a cab company who will give you a rate for driving guests home who might not want to drive themselves.

Remember, the more consideration you show the guests, the more likely it is you will be first to be considered for the next job.

8.   Audio-visual requirements. Can everyone see in a huge meeting room? If not, you'll need to find video vendors who can set up screens, projectors and/or monitors so everyone can see what's happening on the stage. Are Excel or slide shows an integral part of a meeting/pleasure event? You will need the appropriate projectors and equipment to make that happen. Once again, it is good to offer two or three possible companies with prices so the client can choose. It lends the appearance of offering good value for their money.

9.   Decoration requirements. Pay attention to what your client wants in this regard and do not impose your aesthetics on the event. Remember, you are the one working for him or her. But if the client is way off base on, say, a color scheme that clashes, you can find a diplomatic way to tell them this. In short, be the ambassador of good taste but in a tactful manner. And hey, if a Hawaiian theme is what they want, give them the best darned Hawaiian party they will ever have.

10.   Entertainment requirements. This is a wide open door to showcase your creativity. When the client wants a band, remember to look at the age of potential attendees. You will never please everyone, but certain things really do appeal to a majority of people depending on who your crowd is. Maybe you want a stand-up comedian or stage actors. Whatever the case may be, again, focus on what your client wants

(the wish) and make the magic happen by giving him/her what (s)he wants.

11. Exhibition services requirements. Some events might include a convention-like element such as, for example, a trade show or the like. You can count on there being a number of vendors with new and exciting equipment they all want to show off to the client. As such, you want to arrange a suitable space including the various sizes of exhibition spaces. You have to pay careful attention to physical space because you must take into account the flow of foot traffic through the space in between the exhibits.

12. Collateral needs such as valet parking and security services. Many cities have police departments whose officers are allowed to work as security off duty. They will charge you a fee, but at least you have the peace of mind of knowing actual police officers are working ON an event, particularly if it is in a sketchy area in a big city. Again you want to present the client with a few choices and lend the appearance of offering value.

13. Any additional materials/services like layouts, renderings, photos, video footage, information and official documents about your company or business, information about your managing staff, portfolio, references and other information that validates (a) that you are professional, (b) credible and (c) legitimate.

14. And finally, most RFPs specify the due date, to whom you should address your proposal, where to send it for review and what process they will follow to select the

winning bidder. So you want to include a statement of thanks for considering your proposal.

Once you have clarified all of your doubts and received responses to all your questions, you can adjust your proposal to meet the requirements of your client's RFP. You have to focus all your attention on submitting a proposal that is as detailed as possible, but also clear and easy to understand. Address each and every one of the original requirements. You can go beyond the requirements by presenting more than one alternative to each service needed, but shouldn't leave any requirement unaddressed or without an answer.

By providing information about your organization, your past events, references, management curricula and your expertise, you are giving your customer proof that you are professional, know your industry and market and that you are a reliable source. I know I have said this often in previous chapters, but some of the most important things are the photos or videos of past events. These give you instant credibility and allow your customer to see visual images of what you are capable of delivering for him/her. Always carry a digital camera and tripod to document all of your professional work. This, in turn, will help you illustrate the quality and variety of your work on future opportunities.

Before your customer decides whether or not to choose you to be the event planner, (s)he can ask for additional items or revisions to the proposal. You might have to modify something regarding the design, add something for entertainment, take away something from the menu or to revise the price on something. The modifications could be on anything and you have to be flexible to address and meet the new terms.

When asked to adjust your proposal, you must carry out your changes or revisions diligently and show as much interest and flexibility as possible, offering suitable alternatives where necessary, so (s)he can see you are part of his/her team. Show that the event is as important to you as it is for the client.

Keep a track record of all your leads. It's really important to always be at the ready and know how each lead is evolving so you can make the right decisions at the right time to be able to close the sale. I see the sales process like a football game; everything I do correctly is like advancing another yard on the field.

Sometimes you get to advance 10 or 20 yards in one play, but you can also lose yards on the field if you are not aware of what the client is looking for and you fail to provide exactly that. So be alert, don't let bad decisions, negotiations or actions hold you back or even get you a fumble. With my guidance, I cannot promise you a touchdown or goal, but I can sure promise you will gain yards.

That said, be brave and respond to several RFPs. Practice really does improve and the only way to find out how the whole thing works... is to do it.

To gain a better understanding on this topic and benefit from my years of experience, join my insiders list at www. MasteringEventPlanning.com

CHAPTER RECAP

1. Planning is critical, both to the success of events and the overall success of your event planning business. You

must consider all of the logistics that are crucial to preparation and execution; in other words, you must always plan for success.

2. A big part of planning for the success of your event planning business is learning and understanding the basics of sales techniques and strategies, as well as understanding the overall sales process as you follow up on leads.

3. Following up on leads is the foundation of sales success. It can be a long and sometimes difficult process, but is absolutely vital in order to get a customer to make a decision to retain your services. A key task is to prepare and present winning bids and proposals.

4. Preparing winning bids and proposals involves paying attention to details and the specifics of what the client is seeking. In many cases this information will be made available to you in the form of a Request for Proposal (RFP). Make the most of your efforts by being selective about the RFP's to which you respond, selecting only those which best fit your business specialty and for which you are qualified to provide services.

5. Your response to RFPs should contain as much, if not more, detail than the RFP itself. Review the elements of the RFP and be sure your bid response addresses each one specifically and comprehensively. If you have questions about anything in an RFP, contact the issuing company early in the process so you can be sure you are providing the information they need to make their decision.

6. Keep track of all your leads, noting where you are at in the process for each one so you will always be informed and prepared.

CHAPTER 13

SELECTING AND CREATING EVENT THEMES

"All our dreams can come true, if we have the courage to pursue them."

-- Walt Disney

WHY CHOOSE A THEME?

A theme is one of the primary elements that makes an event unforgettable. You can create a theme out of practically any concept or idea you or your customer might have in mind, and you can make that idea a reality by skillfully combining certain elements in the right proportion, sequence and scale.

IMPORTANT

The foundation of any theme can be recreated through the manipulation of various elements such as décor, scenery, costumes, music, games, linens, lighting, food and beverages, entertainment, centerpieces, giveaways, and more.

THEME PARTY VS. THEME EVENT

Before I start explaining how to select and create a memorable theme party or event, I want to make a quick distinction between a theme party and a themed event.

A theme party is usually a one to five-hour-long celebration, organized either by a corporation of some kind, a family or even an individual. It incorporates many of the elements that I have mentioned above to create your concept, taking into account everything from the invitation to the event, to the closing details such as a giveaway or thank you note following the event.

For example, let's say that your client decides to throw a Moroccan theme party at your community country club. She invites all her guests by sending them an original and unique invitation in the form of a flying carpet. When the guests arrive at the venue, a hostess greets them as she hands out a veil for the ladies and a turban for the men. They are immediately impressed with the décor and all other elements through which you created the theme and they have a wonderful time all evening through the combination of entertainment, food, and every little detail that goes to make that night unforgettable.

A theme event, on the other hand, is usually sponsored or organized by a corporation, and is aimed to reach certain objectives set by the company. A theme event can be created by using all elements listed above (décor, scenery, costumes, music, games, linens, lighting, food and beverages, entertainment, centerpieces, giveaways) or by using a focal idea or set of ideas that serves as a guiding concept to inspire actions to reach certain goals. As I said, it could involve either the business idea alone or the business idea combined with the visual and sensory elements mentioned above.

A themed event can also last for a day or more, and might even include a series of events aimed to reach the same objectives. This series of ongoing events, in turn, could last several months or even years to achieve the desired objectives. You also have to find the right title for your themed event.

An example of a themed event created by both a business idea and elements that are visual, sensory, or tangible involves one of my clients who decided to communicate to his employees that the company was ready to take action and embark on conquering the market with their brands.

This company had recently been acquired by another international corporation that was expanding its reach with a global perspective. They had also hired a completely new management team from the very top to high- and middle-management levels. In other words, the company had undergone a complete restructuring at all levels and had spent two years analyzing the market and competition without making much noise... until they approached me to help them enter the market with a bang.

They were both re-launching positioned company brands that had just been acquired, as well as introducing new ones into this frontier territory. So they asked me to develop a theme concept for their corporate convention that could communicate to the attendees what the company was going through and would reinforce the sense of unity amongst all members of the organization. The event was also intended to clarify the scope of the actions to be taken and the dimension of the objectives they were seeking to attain, as well as to motivate the employees to embark on this challenging and difficult endeavor in such a way that they were totally committed to succeed, no matter what.

After reviewing all elements to develop an inclusive guiding concept that could be created using an inspiring idea and visual and sensory theme, I developed an event based on the famous Latin sentence: "VENI, VIDI, VICI" which means, "I came, I saw, I conquered."

With a Roman concept in mind, we played around with the idea that the company was a legion of well-trained centurions who had just come to this battlefield (market) for new victories (sales); ("Veni").

During the short time they had been in the market, they had developed a vision and strategy and had created an ambitious plan of attack; ("Vidi").

So, by the time of the event, they were preparing to proceed to "attack" hard and achieve the ambitious goals they had set for themselves which consisted of beating the competition and conquering their market; ("Vici").

Since this Latin phrase was coined by General Julius Caesar and was used to describe the victories of Rome at the Battle of Zela, it seemed a relevant concept because it allowed us to work with a plethora of decoration, musical and entertainment elements, as well as with the actual idea of planning and following a campaign to the letter in order to triumph.

We turned the stage into a coliseum, the podium became a Roman chariot and we embellished the whole thing to create the appropriate ambience by using elements from ancient Rome like banners with imperial insignia, columns and props.

All the signage for the event was made in a "Latin style" font and the music to start every general session consisted of fanfares and trumpets. One of the outdoor activities we organized was called "the Gladiators' Challenge," into which we brought all kinds of battle-like inflatable games and implemented tournaments in which the teams of attendees challenged each other to fight a duel. Of course, during the three-day event everything from invitations, badges, boards, and settings had to do with the main theme.

As you can see, you can have a theme out of practically any concept or idea you or your customer might have in mind. The only two things you need to integrate are the objectives and the guiding concept. After that, you need to combine certain ingredients in the right quantity, sequence, and scale.

As a farewell night, we organized a sophisticated toga party that we called "The Triumph." We had a couple of Roman characters greet the guests, dancers and acrobats as entertainers, a champagne fountain, and all the waiters were wearing a centurion helmet. The hotel was in charge of serving a truly magnificent and decadent buffet.

"Veni, Vidi, Vici" resulted in a concept that referred not only to victory but to celebration of high achievements that brought to mind a world of great deeds and characters. That is why it was perfect as a guiding concept to carry out our event.

Every element of the convention related to our theme—the logo, the slogan, the invitations, the badges, the stage, the characters some of the top executives impersonated, as well as the speeches. Even the presentations and activities showed some aspect of the theme; it appeared in the audiovisual support (jingles or videos), special effects, the venue, the costumes, giveaways, music, entertainment, outdoor team building activities, the cocktail reception and all theme party functions, right up to the farewell dinner.

Therefore, rather than implementing only sensory and tangible elements as one usually does with a theme party held purely for fun, a themed corporate event is used more as a method of conveying an idea or set of values that the company embraces to its audience (be it employees, customers or suppliers). The event is used as the vehicle to implement many communication resources and make it easier for attendees to understand at an experiential, emotional level so they can make it their own.

I only want to add that when you plan a theme event, you should make sure you can follow through before, during, and after the event (as in the theme parties). Your theme should also be complemented by the tone and content of your presentations, so make sure you let the speakers know about the theme and how they can incorporate it into their remarks without overusing it. A themed event should have as many elements strung together as possible to create a real ambience while achieving the client's objectives.

The most important thing for you now is to understand the distinction I just discussed between themed parties and themed corporate events, and to be able to come up with creative, intelligent and practical ideas to develop a theme from the production point of view.

SELECTING AND CREATING THE RIGHT THEME

So, let's get back to selecting and creating the right theme from the perspective that interests us.

Since the purpose of this book is to help you understand, as much as possible, the most important logistic and creative factors involved in an event planning business, I think it is proper to devote this space to the steps and things you have to take in consideration to create a theme party or event from a production perspective, rather than an entrepreneurial or management philosophy.

FACT:

Few people really know how expensive producing a quality theme party or event can be, especially one that includes most of the elements I've just listed above.

That said, from the perspective of an event planner, what elements can you use to create a theme? One of the first things you have to consider before you start is your budget.

There's a huge difference between two events for 500 people each, with one of them valued at $40,000 and the other one at $100,000. In the first case, the cost per person would be $80 and in the second case it would be $200, more than twice as much as the other. And this cost difference can occur regardless of whether the two events include the same number of items or services in their production. This means that sometimes you can hire third party suppliers specialized in every service you need for your event, and some other times you need to rely on the hotel's or the venue's props (if they have any) and their linens, centerpieces, and supplies.

When you have a decent budget, you can be very creative, but when you don't, you have to be even more creative, believe me.

So, the good news is that regardless of the amount of money you have for an event, as long as you have a minimum and reasonable budget you still can throw extraordinary and affordable theme events. You just have to learn how to transform some everyday items into spectacular and visual decorative elements for your events. Sometimes you have enough money to hire a specialist in event décor and have a custom made design, other times you'll have to work with whatever resources and props the hotel or venue may have for its customers. Either way, you have to be creative and get the most out of your budget to make your customers happy.

If you want some good tips on ideas and resources for how to create a memorable theme party or event, go to www.MasteringEventPlanning.com, where as a member you can access our tips section on how-to's for invitations, entertainment, room makeovers, games and activities, décor, table settings, centerpieces, and much more.

When I create a theme party or event, I look for inspiring ideas in many places, such as movies, television, bizbash, and blogs from experts in our industry. I also read magazines like the Special Event magazine, *Event Solutions*, department store catalogues, Crate and Barrel, *Architectural Digest*, and any lifestyle magazine that covers events of the rich and famous for more ideas. Everywhere you go you can find sources of inspiration and ideas for your events, such as at flea markets or bazaars and themed boutiques. Even a trip or going to the theater can inspire a concept for a theme event.

Take into consideration both big and small details, but remember that the difference between a regular, well-organized event and an extraordinary one lies in the details. So, stay attentive to detail, go for the little touches that make the big differences, but recognize that you have to go for it more than once, probably twice, thrice or more. So, be a detail-oriented event planner when creating the right theme.

Remember, when you are on a tight budget, your brain and creativity have to go beyond the everyday. That is, it has to go big, free, open, out of the box, into another completely different box, so open your eyes and learn as much as possible about how you can turn little ideas into big and original creations for events.

Just be careful and don't spend your entire budget in an attempt to impress your clients and guests. It is super important not to forget that this activity of yours is a business and not a hobby. As such, it has to produce income for you, not only satisfaction and applause.

Also, be smart when you work on a budget (a tight budget). This means using your resources intelligently, instead of trying to fill up the room or the space with oversize props and decorative elements. Put all your eggs in one basket and go for one grand element or prop as the main focal point of your theme and place it at the center of attention, in one spot, not many. That would be enough to create a theme.

REMEMBER...

Don't be afraid to try out-of-the-ordinary and crazy ideas; almost any such idea can be successfully implemented when designing and creating events. Just make sure it is viable to do it, as well as safe.

One of my secrets for creating great theme parties and events that my customers and guests still praise years later lies in always wanting to try different ideas. I did not want to do the same thing more than three times, so I was always on the lookout for crazy ideas, convincing my clients to go and try them. That kept me motivated, full of energy and always looking forward to the next challenge. Today, we as event producers are obliged to be more creative and efficient so we can do more with less, without compromising the originality and quality of our creations.

Push your limits and those of your customers, otherwise neither of you will have as much fun, and after a while both you and your customer will lose interest in doing more events together.

Everywhere you go, open your eyes. There is always an idea sitting there, waiting for you to see it. Ask for references for entertainment options, go to modern art museums, go to trade shows, and when in a hotel take a look to see if there's any event going on to get ideas from whatever interesting and original things they might be doing.

So, any time you organize a theme party or theme event, make sure you have the five senses considered: the look, the scent, the sound, the touch and the taste. Special events and theme parties should not necessarily be elegant; they just have to be extraordinary. And whatever you do, make it fun and surprising.

When developing a theme, think of the following items to consider your décor ideas and entertainment:

- Entertainment

- Costumes

- Entrance/foyer

- Table settings

- Centerpieces, floral or themed

- Main stage

- Plants and trees

- Living decor in the form of interactive characters

- Artisans

- Fabrics and drapes

- Decoration around the venue

- Flower arrangements

- Buffet/menu

- Drinks

- Wait staff (waiters and waitresses) in costumes or accessories to be characterized according to the theme (a hat, a shirt, etc).

- Recorded music

- Live music

- Audiovisual resources

- Lighting

- Interactive activities

- Performers

- Party favors

- Giveaways at the end of the event

If your budget allows for all these items, make sure they are all related to your theme.

Remember that ideas for a theme party can come from many places. Here are just a few:

- Movies (*Avatar*, *Indiana Jones*, *James Bond*)

- Colors (pink passion, black and white, red extravaganza)

- Countries and places (Mexican Fiesta, Brazilian Carnival, Ancient Egypt)

- Holidays (Mardi Gras, St Patrick's, Halloween)

- Seasons (spring, summer fest)

- Decades (fabulous fifties, flower power-60s, Disco Night 70s, Eighties, Charleston's 20s)

- Music (rhythm of the night, jazz night, rock your party, salsa ball).

A theme party can consist of various elements, but you can always differentiate or categorize it by considering the main feature that inspired it in the first place, and for that you just have to see the list above as an example, and determine which one is the main element: a color, a movie, a country, a season, etc.

But there is much more to work from when finding and developing the perfect theme for the occasion. Ideas can also come from cartoons, novels, or tales. You can also have themes that are based on region, sports, religion, esoteric concepts, TV shows, science, fiction, interactive activities, costume, birthday and anniversary milestones, nature, geography, life milestones and many others.

As I said at the beginning of this section, you can create a theme out of practically any idea. If you wish to see a complete list of themes in each of these categories and a detailed description of what each theme includes, you can do so at www.MasteringEventPlanning.com, where as a member you can access a complete list of more than 50 different themes to get ideas on how you can create your unique events.

I always ask myself why there are fewer and fewer original and unforgettable parties. I remember how, in the beginning of my career in the event planning industry, my business started to gain recognition and prestige for the simple fact that we were organizing truly unforgettable parties. They were events which left guests feeling fortunate to have attended and with unforgettable memories. I positioned my business as the best alternative in our market to throw the most magnificent and enjoyable events from the very first day I started it.

One reason why there are fewer unforgettable events and parties is that we live in a more rushed world, with less time to devote to having fun without any particular reason. But we also have more time to become conscious of too many things all at once. Or perhaps it is that this fascinating profession which consists of inspiring, visualizing, creating and delivering the "best party or event ever" for both our clients and their guests has made us believe that the key factor to turn a common celebration into an unforgettable event, is to merely please our customer by providing him/her with flawless, precise, unique and efficient event planning services so we can make her feel like "another guest."

Well, yes, we live in a rushed world with less time to devote to having fun just for the sake of celebrating life. And yes, I actually believe that pleasing our customers is really important, if not crucial, to guarantee the viability of any event planning business; even more so if we consider the competitive and harsh commercial environment in which we currently perform.

To create moments that your guests will remember forever, I strongly suggest that you first understand that throwing a party or organizing an event for any reason is not, and it has never been, about the host in his position as the customer. Instead, it is about him as the host and, most importantly, his guests whom he has assured will experience a unique, memorable and enjoyable event.

But despite the popular and undisputable belief that making your client feel like "another guest" to his/her own party is the most important factor to turn a common celebration into an unforgettable party, that's actually not what makes an event unforgettable, even when it's imperative to the viability of your business.

Therefore, besides being an extremely professional service provider, my personal opinion is that to turn a common celebration into an unforgettable event, you must focus all of your attention and energy on providing creative and unique elements that trigger your guests' emotions and make their hearts resonate with the many moods of any special occasion. You have to aim at every one of the senses.

An out-of-the-ordinary and memorable theme party or event should have all elements communicating the same message, through all 5 senses, harmoniously, flawlessly and always considering the surprise factor. So go for it and create a great event. After all, isn't unmatched style what a truly special event should provide?

If this aspect is particularly important for you, you should review my web site www.sarao.com.mx - where you'll find photos and videos of the most popular theme parties and events I offer my clients.

CHAPTER RECAP

1. A great theme is one of the primary components of a successful and memorable event. With just a bit of creativity, you can create an amazing theme out of just about any idea or concept put forth by you or your client.

2. Understand the differences between a theme party and a theme event and apply this knowledge to create the solutions your clients want and deserve. Work with your clients to make sure you understand what they desire and then put together the right elements to fulfill those desires and exceed their expectations.

3. Selecting and creating the right theme must be done from the production perspective in order to put together the elements that best accomplish this goal. It all starts with the budget, which is the biggest determining factor in putting together the right assortment of elements to create the theme successfully.

4. Review the list of elements that can contribute to the theme, including décor, entertainment, music, food, and games or other activities. Look for theme ideas all around you and in every place imaginable; often time the very best ideas come from the most unexpected and "outside the box" sources.

5. Creating an out-of–the-ordinary and memorable theme event is all about making sure all elements of the event communicate the same message, using all five senses and putting everything together in a way that's harmonious and flawless.

WORKBOOK

This section gathers all the tips, pointers and excercises I have mentioned before for your easy reference. You can take some sheets of paper or open a text file on your computer to take matters into your own hands and really commit to paper your ideas on how you are going to start becoming a successful event planner – today. Use the guidelines I have provided and adapt them to your own circumstances.

SELF-ASSESSMENT CAREER PLANNER: EVENT PLANNING PROFESSIONAL

Answer each of these questions completely and honestly. There is no measurement scale for scoring your answers and there is no single right answer to each question. Rather, your answers to all of these questions, taken together, will reveal to you some key insights into whether or not a career as an event planning professional is right for you.

1. Are you willing to work hard every day?   This means focusing on customer service and looking for every answer, and even improvising to deal with the obstacles that will arise day after day; be willing to put in long hours when necessary, working late at night or even on weekends, sometimes not being able to spend enough time with your family and those you love; and having the drive to succeed no matter what, be willing to deal with frustration and move forward.

2. Do you have a business mindset?   This means continuously putting business needs at the forefront of everything you do, striving to sell, to create income and to be passionate about success. You have to be willing to step out of your "comfort zone" and start striving to understand and learn everything that you don't know yet, but that you need to master to be able to perform an outstanding role as an event planning professional.

3. Do you have a creative mindset?   This means being willing to take a simple idea and build upon it to create something special, turning the "everyday" experience into an "extraordinary" event. Are you skilled at catching every detail in the surroundings? For example, do you look at details when watching a movie, walking around your neighborhood, looking at a furniture catalog or décor magazine, stepping into a department store, boutique, gallery or museum? Can you start from a simple detail and create a whole visual concept out of it?

4. Which of the following characteristics apply to you?

- You like being surrounded by people

- You don't mind working longer hours

- You are an organized individual

- You like coordinating a lot of tasks and people at the same time

- You enjoy fulfilling the needs of others as an essential part of your job

- You are willing to take the risk of starting your own business and do whatever it needs to achieve the rewards of success

5. When you discover in yourself a weakness or a skill that needs improvement, what do you do? This is all about understanding your own tendencies and reactions when faced with something about yourself that's not as fully developed as it could be. To be successful in this business you need to face weaknesses head on in order to resolve them, rather than ignoring them, pushing them aside or just leaving them as they are and hoping for the best.

6. What are your personal goals for your event planning business? The answers to this question reveal a great deal about your personality, your motivation, your enthusiasm and your passion for this business. Remember that we cannot reach our goals if we don't know where we are going. So please answer this question: Where do you want to get with this business? What do you what to achieve in your life? Be as specific as possible. You can say that you want a business that allows you to live the lifestyle that you are looking for, and that you are searching for the freedom of being your own boss, etc. Whatever your objectives are, try to clarify them in this section so that you can reach them.

CHECKLIST: YOUR SKILLS, ATTRIBUTES AND ATTITUDES

You are solely responsible for generating your leads and finding potential clients. The following statements represent critical skills, attributes and attitudes you must possess to be successful on this task. I recommend you to read these skills, attributes and attitudes carefully, and write down next to each one a brief description of how you are going to ensure they become an inherent part of the way you do business each and every day.

1. **Be accessible at all times.** You have to provide a contact method (that could be your e-mail, your mobile phone, etc.) where your clients and potential clients will be able to find you when they need you.

2. **Keep your promises.** Don't promise more than what you can actually deliver, because you will find yourself in trouble when the clients claim for what you promised and didn't give. However, if there is something that you are sure you can offer your clients, mention it, and promise it. And of course, always try to give more than what you have promised (remember this is my secret formula for success).

3. **Respond to your e-mail, and phone messages the day they arrive.** It is very important to be expecting your customers' and potential customers' communications, since every contact opportunity is a selling opportunity, and you cannot let the clients decide that they need to find elsewhere (your competition) the answers to their questions because you don't answer when they need you. I suggest you have two specific shifts along the day to dedicate yourself only to answering to your emails and phone messages; but be careful: avoid distracting yourself from doing other business activities just because you spend too much time answering your customers' communications.

4. **Acknowledge your mistakes and do something to resolve them.** Being capable of understanding that you are wrong is essential for enhancing your services and making your business grow. Maybe you can't know from the start everything that your customer needs, but you can pay close attention to their reactions when some of your suggestions seem not to be the best choice, and ask for their opinions to realize when it is necessary to improve or change your strategy to avoid making the same mistakes.

5. **Always be punctual.** Punctuality is a sign of respect and professionalism, and respecting your client's time is one of the keys to keep them satisfy and happy about making business with someone like you.

6. **Follow up when you say you will and when your client expects you to.** As you know, the follow-up process is critical to know where you are positioned in relation to each client, and to find the right solution at the right time. Remember: good results for your business and your sales depend on your follow-up work.

7. **Be disciplined; wake up early and at the same time every day.** Discipline helps you being persistent, because it keeps you focused on your goals. And, as you know, perseverance is the key to success, in this and every other business.

8. **Establish a routine; exercise, take regular breaks during the day, don't go to bed late and pamper yourself whenever you feel like you've earned it.** All these aspects are related to your mental and physical health, an area that we frequently overlook in our efforts to generate more and more income. Income is essential for your business to keep operating, but your health is essential for you to keep operating; and if you don't feel good, surely your business will start going down too.

CHECKLIST: KEY BUSINESS REQUIREMENTS

The following items are key business requirements that you must carefully consider and decide upon. Use this checklist to go through each requirement in detail, writing down the information you need to make a final decision. You can review Chapter 4 to get more information about each topic below.

1. Choose your business structure

-- Sole Proprietorship?

-- General Partnership?

-- Incorporation?

-- Limited Liability Company (LLC) or Limited Liability Partnership (LLP)?

2. Legal considerations
(Please notice that this is not a recommendation; this information I am sharing with you is not meant to be a consultancy or anything similar, it is just to remind you that you need to make an in-depth investigation of your options and take the best decision to give a structure to your business.)

-- Select a legal advisor; sooner or later you will need the answers to questions of legal nature that affect your business.

-- Look for someone with experience related to event planning businesses to be your mentor and advisor, and to help you answer the questions that will surely arise along the way.

3. Accounting and taxes

-- Select a qualified professional accountant

-- Review and understand all accounting choices and decisions; you must have at least basic knowledge on this subject to be able to take the right decisions.

-- Understand deductible and non-deductible expenses according to the tax laws applicable to your business.

-- Establish a regular schedule of communications with your accountant

-- Ensure accountant stays up to date on all tax regulations and changes, and informs you about those changes as soon as they come up.

4. Zoning requirements

-- You must verify everything related to zoning since the beginning, to be sure that you are fulfilling all the requirements. Can you legally operate a home-based business from your location?

-- Remember that starting a home-based event planning business is not going to run into zoning issues in most places if you do not have customers, vendors or suppliers coming to and from your business location on a regular basis, and if you don't keep an inventory of equipment going constantly out and into your house; I mean, as long as you don't use your space in a commercial manner, you are generally going to be okay regarding zoning.

-- However, check with local authorities for current zoning requirements to be sure that you are not avoiding your obligations.

-- Remember, failure to abide by zoning requirements may trigger some fairly hefty penalties –ranging from monetary fees to immediately having to halt business operations until zoning issues are resolved–, and it can also lead to problems with your neighbors.

-- You need to verify that your neighbors and your apartment manager don't have any issue with the fact that a resident is establishing a home-based business. Again, normally this will not be a problem as long as you run your business without using your space in a commercial manner.

5. Business insurance

Decide which business insurance option is better for your needs and get it as soon as possible. Below you will see some of the most common options, although you will not find the same products and insurance in all countries and states, and dispositions may vary from one place to another. So carry on your own investigation and take the best decision for your business. But foremost: do not stay without coverage; you need to have one or more business insurances:

-- General Liability

-- Product Liability

-- Home-Based Business

-- Worker's Compensation

-- Business Interruption

Consult with business insurance professional to determine best combination of types and coverage for your needs.

6. Local permits

Take the time to investigate and solve the following issues:

-- What types of special circumstances require permits to do a particular event or to operate your business?

-- Who is the proper local authority to consult on permit issues?

7. Taking customer payments

The most common payment methods in the event planning business are:

- Bank transfer or deposit

- Checks

- Credit Cards

- Cash

To be able to receive deposits you need to open a bank account and have always at hand: your account number, Swift code and Routing number. Cash payment is not common in this industry, although there are some last minute services that the client pays in cash. On the other hand, accepting credit cards is the best choice for processing payments quickly and conveniently.

Do you want to use a third party credit card processing service? Paypal is a great way to pay and receive payments by using a credit card; it's easy to get, fast and safe to process. Or do you want to set up your own merchant credit card account via your bank or credit union? Write down the advantages/disadvantages of either choice and make the best decision.

Remember that the easier and more convenient it is for customers to pay you, the faster you will see money deposited into your bank account.

CHECKLIST: IDENTIFY YOUR CORE SERVICES AND DESIGN YOUR ACTION PLAN

The following items are topics that require some additional thought and effort to evaluate in detail. Use this checklist to go through each topic, writing down the information you need to then make a final decision. Focus on being very clear about your goals, setting them up to be attainable, accountable and achievable within a realistic time frame. You can return to Chapter 5 to get deeper into the topic of each of the questions below.

1. Are you going to be an event planning generalist or specialist? Write down reasons for and against each choice, paying special attention to your own skills and preferences, as well as the marketplace demands in your area.

2. Are you going to be an event services supplier? Write down reasons for and against this choice, carefully considering the business advantages and disadvantages you might experience. And mention what event services you will provide.

3. What type of service or product do you provide in the event planning industry? Define it as clearly as possible. Ask yourself the following question: What type(s) of event(s) will you like the most to plan? The most common types of events that a professional event planner can specialize in are: corporate events, private parties, fundraising events, theme parties, weddings, family events and children's parties, etc. I do not recommend specializing in more than two of these areas; however, this doesn't mean that occasionally you can do events that step out of your specialty area.

4. How are your clients going to find out about you? Establish marketing strategies: e-mail campaigns, website, word of mouth, etc. Review every resource that you could use, and choose the most efficient ones and those that better fit your budget... remember that it is all about spreading the word that you exist, to the larger possible number of people, but without costing you a fortune.

5. Is there a market for your services? Identify and check the competition, whether your targeted potential clients are already buying their services and, if possible, what prices they are paying. Create a list of media where you have found ads from your potential competitors, and if possible, identify your competitors by their names and make a list of those names to know who they are, and to be able to offer a better service and make customers choose you instead of them.

6. What sets you apart from the competition? Price, quality of service, general expertise, service variety, creativity, specialization, etc.? Choose one or two of these attributes, and ensure you distinguish yourself because of that; don't try to cover all attributes, you cannot excel in every area. Also, I do not recommend you to distinguish yourself by the price; in this business this can be a problem rather than an advantage, because you can leave profitability behind and never generate profits because you chose to distinguish your business by offering the lowest price. A better option would be choosing to be the one that offers more for the same amount of money; in that case, make sure that all extras are valuable for the client but don't need a considerable outlay. Instead, look for things that don't cost you in money, but that represent a valuable extra task, equipment from your inventory that you offer your client for free, etc. There are many ways of creating value to distinguish from the competition, without having to put in large amounts of money.

7. What are your monthly fixed costs? Remember not to leave anything out. Consider, for example, service fees for hosting your website, payment for having a corporate e-mail, cost of Internet access, and all expenses once your business has come to life.

8. How will you determine appropriate pricing for your services? In order to start, you can carry on an investigation asking the competition for their prices to be able to measure the market value of the services that you offer. Keep in mind that it is not easy to operate this business with a fixed price list that you hand to all your clients. From my experience, I can tell you that it just doesn't work, because no two events are exactly alike, so there are many variables that can affect your costs. However, you can use basic rates for each service, which will serve as a parameter to quote faster in each case. Also keep in mind the following considerations mentioned in detail in Chapter 5:

-- Review the factors affecting what constitutes the right price for your services

-- Move away from the "man hours = reasonable price" mentality

-- Understand the three suggested ways to determine the right price to charge (research the competition, research client expenditures, consult with local business organizations and associations)

-- Balance your pricing between being too cheap and too expensive, keeping in mind that it's okay to charge more if you consistently deliver higher value to your clients.

9. Which pricing method(s) will you use for each case?

As explained in Chapter 5, there are several methods from which you can choose when it comes to charging the right price for your services. These methods are:

-- **By the project:** to set your price by the project, once you have calculated your fixed costs and variable costs, the next step is to add in your associated profit margin. Profit margin is typically set at some specific percentage above the total costs (fixed + variable).

-- **By fixed price (for additions):** there are additional costs or services that were not initially foreseen by both parties in the original deal, and in such cases you will usually deal with these additional costs by adding a fixed price or surcharge for the additional item(s).

-- **By flat fee:** as an event planning professional, you can take a flat fee approach, but you should only agree to this kind of arrangement if the client commits to using your services on an ongoing, pre-determined basis.

-- **Based on commission:** you can make money off supplier/vendor commissions: i) each time you hire them for an event you're coordinating, or ii) for referring them to other clients who end up making a purchase. In both cases, the supplier collects the total amount of the sale price and, subsequently, pays you some percentage (the commission) of that price you both agreed upon. It is critical, however, that the supplier or vendor you work with or recommend is someone reliable whom you truly trust.

-- **Using discounts:** using discounts is a reduction in the price a service supplier charges you, that is to say, the supplier reduces their price by an agreed-upon percentage and charges you this reduced price. You are able to make money by charging your client a mark-up which is equal to or a little higher than the original price of your supplier; in other words, you charge your client the regular price for this part of the event and do not pass along the discount. Then you end up making more money and the client ends up paying almost the regular price of that service.

-- **Using mark-ups of other services:** remember that it is generally not a good idea to charge your clients an agency fee or percentage of all services confirmed, and a mark-up; charge either one or the other, not both.

-- **By the hour:** bill by the hour is the worst idea, even though some jobs are priced this way, for example: a guitarist, a mime, etc. I recommend you to avoid this pricing method, since it is extremely difficult to accurately estimate the number of hours you will dedicate to a project.

My advice is that you use this system:

Charge all items by unit price, and offer a global price for all your event services; or offer global prices for service bundles, for example: a global price for the whole closing event decoration or a global price for the whole event entertainment, instead of breaking down every little item. If you offer bundle prices, normally the final price will be less than the sum of all the originally separate services.

There are services, like catering, that are commonly offered based on the number of people attending the event, but once the number of assistants is established, there are venues that negotiate an all-inclusive price (generally hotels) so you can offer your client that all-inclusive price per person... in this particular case, you get your profit by negotiating a commission or discount for you with the caterer or the hotel, and not adding a margin –since that can complicate things a lot–; it is better to be transparent and give the client the real price (the real price is the price they offer you before negotiating your commission).

In the other cases, when selling other types of event services, I do not recommend working by commission, since it really limits your chances of covering your costs and hence profitability.

You should analyze when it is better to offer a proposal with each and every item charged separately, when to offer global prices for service bundles, and when to offer a global price for the whole event.

10. What are your income expectations vs. needs? Be realistic about how much you want to make at any point in time versus what you need to make at any point in time. You can return to Chapter 3 to get a better idea of how to go through this exercise. It is okay defining your income expectations and following that goal, but don't forget that this process takes some time and requires a lot of effort, so you have to be persistent. Remember: perseverance is the key in this and every other business.

11. How much do you need to sell to break even? To be able to answer this question you need to figure out how much you would need to charge in order to merely break even on the costs. Breaking even, of course, means you don't make any profit; so making a "break even" analysis is just the starting point to determine the profit margin necessary to create a profit for your business.

12. How much do you need to sell to generate your expected income? To answer this question you need to know the estimated costs for the different events or services that you offer. Remember to review Section "Pricing Your Services" in Chapter 5 of this book.

13. How are you going to sell that quantity and in what timeframe are you going to sell it? When answering this question it is vital to be realistic. Why? Because if you are not realistic you set yourself up for failure by aiming for goals that are too high to accomplish in a very short period of time. I remind you again, that perseverance is the key; sometimes, when we don't get immediate results, we see everything in a very negative way and we start believing that we are not in the right way or that our endeavor will not work, that we will not be able to succeed. But this is not true. If you seriously put your mind to it and take action decisively, there is no way that you end up not achieving your desired success.

14. What will you consider when creating a project budget? Remember that the most important thing is planning an event that fits within the client's budget. For an accurate budget you need to consider every possible expense, no matter how small or minor. Use a detailed spreadsheet to track every expense and always make sure that you are receiving your well-earned gains. Don't ever work for free.

CHECKLIST: FIVE KEY ACTIONS FOR SUCCESS

Through my 20+ years of experience (as well as a great deal of early trial and error), I have discovered there are five key actions necessary to generate business and create success. Answer each of the following questions/statements to identify how to best put these actions to use in your business to create success. You can review all these topics on Chapter 3.

1. Define a target audience, your potential clients, because if you can't define them, you can't find them. Who is your ideal client? Establish a profile for each type of client (if targeting your services to more than one type). I don't suggest you to target your services to more than two types of clients, at least not at the beginning.

2.   Figure out what your client base loves and hates when organizing special events. To find out what your clients want, look at your competition: What are they offering? What are they trying to say to their clients between the lines about what they are offering, beyond their service itself? Ask them: What is it that you most enjoy when organizing special events? And make sure that you offer exactly that (provided it is within your means) or just ask your clients what they hate when organizing events, and see how you can help them solve that issue if they decide to hire you. Ask these questions once and again to all your clients, and pay a lot of attention to their answers; this is the key to offering attractive solutions.

3. Reach your clients with an appealing message, telling them how they can get what they wish or avoid that particular thing they hate. To build this message, the first question that you have to be able to answer is the following: Why would your clients want to do business with you and how would they benefit by doing so? As mentioned in the previous point, you have to find out what your clients value and hate when organizing events.

4. Present yourself and your services as the key to obtaining the dream event they are longing for. Pretend you are doing a half-length pitch to a client for your niche event. What will you say to make them hire you on the spot? Once you are clear about what the client wants and does not want, and have figured out how you can actually give them those things that they want and avoid giving them those that they don't want, then you will be ready to create your sales pitch. Remember that you have to create three different sales pitches, as mentioned in Chapter 6 of this book.

5. Think BIG; become an expert. Do what you know and know what you do like no one else. Do not forget that to place yourself as an expert you not only must know your business in detail –as well as your clients' businesses and industries and the processes and policies that move their businesses– but you have to provide more information about your services and the industry in general, whether sending a newsletter, creating your own blog, participating in online forums, or giving conferences to different audiences about your area of expertise. This will create an immediate communication channel that will help you gain your customers' trust.

CHECKLIST: PREPARE YOUR SALES PITCH

A sales pitch is a communication tool or message used to present information about your business that is designed to inform the listener, initiate consideration of using your services and set the stage for closing the sale.

1. Think about an answer to the following questions as you develop and prepare your sales pitch. You can get deeper into these topics by reviewing Chapter 6.

- What needs are you solving?

- What are the key features of your solution?

- What are the most important benefits that your client receives?

- Why should the potential customer choose your products and services and not those from the competition?

2. Now write down your full 2 to 3 minutes length sales pitch, including those ideas that came up from your answers to the previous questions. The most important thing about a sales pitch is that your clients identify themselves with your speech and feel it as a tailored solution for their needs; that they feel that what they are looking for is exactly what you are offering them and in the way that you are offering it. Your solution must be a tailored suit; exactly what your client is looking for. Therefore, a good pitch is the result of carrying on a thorough investigation of what your potential clients want and do not want when organizing an event, and the pitch summaries it in an attractive way, that resonates with your customers' desires.

3. Condense your full length sales pitch into a half length sales pitch, no more than 1 minute in length. See what the most important ideas are: the most convincing and most responsive to the needs of your target audience, and join them in such a way as to generate a clear message that captures your client attention. This pitch is useful, for example, to start a presentation to your customers (perhaps in a meeting room) and to capture your audience attention, making them interested in what you have to say.

4. Condense your half length sales pitch into a 30 second length ("elevator pitch") sales pitch. Summarizing ideas requires your effort of actually finding the keywords that will create the message; you can say little with a lot of words or you can say much with only a few words. In this case, it is important that every word that you include in your "elevator pitch" is attractive for your audience and generates positive associations in their minds about the importance of hiring your services to achieve the best results.

5. Practice all three of your sales pitches out loud; do so in front of a mirror, in front of trusted friends or relatives and in front of a video camera. If you have no experience with public speaking, it is normal that at first you will not achieve the desired results; you can talk too fast and not pronounce each word clearly, you can get stuck in the middle of your speech, or you can feel shame and convey little confidence. Keep practicing until all three sales pitches are committed to memory and sound completely natural when you share them with others. Practice will help you to feel more confident and to define the proper timing for the speech, so that it is not too slow or too fast, allowing you to pronounce each word properly and to manage different atmospheres to avoid sounding monotonous and boring (but instead being interesting and compelling). Be careful: your speech must never sound untruthful, exaggerated, or memorized; instead, it must seem completely natural, although you have rehearsed it a hundred times. Remember that you can change your pitch if the preferences of your clients change.

CHECKLIST: YOUR MARKETING PLAN

1. Think about the three key principles to succeed in your business. For each principle, write down what it means to you and how you will apply it in your daily business activities. You can review Chapter 8 for further guideline.

-- **Finish what you start.** Do you usually finish what you start? Or do you get bored easily? Or perhaps you get frustrated when something requires a lot of hard work and dedication, and you leave the task unfinished. Keep in mind that if you want to succeed in your event planning business, you need to be focused and determined, and finish what you start. At the same time, be careful and do not confuse this statement with being meticulous; being too exhaustive in the first stage of your endeavor can really be a problem, since your ambition for detail can lead you –without you notice– to avoid finishing whatever you start.

To begin with, you can create a list of the first steps that you want to start and finish in your new event planning business, and you can determine an estimated timeframe for each step and for the tasks involved. But most important is taking the first step; it doesn't need to be "the best first step possible", and you don't have to get uptight about the famous question: "Where do I start? What should I do first? Shall I do this or that? Forget about these questions that will not get you nothing and will only delay your success. Simply define an action and get to work! Do not forget: there is no substitute for decisive action.

-- **Keep it simple.** This complements the previous statement. Simplicity allows you to set achievable goals and go straight to the point.

Review your previous list and see if you have been simple enough when defining the first steps that you want to start and finish in your new business. See if you can simplify even more each of the ideas on your list, so that it helps you set the goals clearly in your mind.

-- **Design it to win the business game.** Remember that this means that your action plan must focus on producing as much income as possible, while at the same time you build the highest possible value for you clients.

Write down the things that you think that will create value for your client. The value can be given by an excellent quality of your product or service, by an outstanding customer service, by unique and innovative ideas, by extra services, or a combination of these or many other variables. What do you think would be your best formula to generate the kind of value that your clients appreciate?

2. Think about the three universal areas of focus (marketing, production and operations). Create a sample calendar for a one week period that reflects the recommended division of effort among these three areas.

Marketing – 60%

Production – 20%

Operations – 20%

Don't forget to review the definitions of these three areas to get a clear idea of what they mean. You can review the section regarding this topic on Chapter 8.

CHECKLIST: PRE-EVENT PLANNING

Review the following key questions to ask each client in the very beginning of the event planning process. Use this checklist to record client answers to these questions; it will help you bring your event to life. Add additional questions as needed based on your particular requirements and those of your clients; you can use Chapter 9 as a guide.

1. Where will the event take place?

2. What kind of event are we talking about? Why are they celebrating? What are the goals?

3. Who is the event for?

4. How many guests will be attending?

5. What percentage of attendees are male, and what percentage of attendees are female?

6. Are your guests primarily couples or singles?

7. Will most of your guests attend with their families/companion?

8. What is the average age of the guests?

9. Do the guests know each other?

10. Are the guests from the local community or are they from out of town?

11. Do the guests work for the same company?

12. When will the event take place? At what time?

13. What is the client's real, actual budget (not the "wish list" or "maybe" budget)?

CHECKLIST: KEY QUESTIONS TO ASK WHEN CREATING A TIMELINE

Ask yourself these questions and record the answers on this checklist. Add additional questions as needed based on your particular requirements.

The answers to these questions will allow you to keep track of everything you need to include in your preliminary timeline of the event. You should be able to figure out estimated timeframes to assess the viability of your timeline, and you must use your organizational skills to arrange everything within your agenda in a logical order. You can refer to Chapter 9 where this topic was discussed.

1. On what day of the week will the event happen?

2. What are you serving at the event?

3. Will the guests be moving from one point to another within the parameters of your venue?

4. What kind of entertainment will you have and how long will each act last?

5. Will speeches be given?

6. How will you deal with requests from speakers?

7. Will a video be presented?

8. Will you have celebrities, official guests, security escorts or the like?

9. Will you need a band for dancing music or use a DJ?

10. Will you require any special equipment?

THANKS TO THE READER

On closing, I would just like to offer my sincere thanks to you, the reader, for taking the time to read my book. I hope that the material contained within it and the benefit of my many years in the event planning business will prove to be of immense use to you in the future.

Of course, this may just be the beginning of your exciting adventure into the magical world of event planning, in which case you will almost certainly want to access further resources to help you on your way. To this end, I invite you to check my website at EventPlanningInsider.com, where you will find a whole range of additional material, including a complete set of manuals on topics ranging from how to organize fun games and interactive events, to how to market and sell your services. In addition, the site contains marketing tools and business management in general that will help you to address all of the important areas that you need to know about in order to set up and run your own successful event planning business.

Having come to the end of this book, I hope that you will appreciate the considerable time and effort which has gone into creating it and so I would request that you demonstrate your respect by not sharing or distributing it, in whole or in part, without my permission. Thank you.

Finally, it just remains for me to wish you the very best of luck. Like any business, event planning presents its own set of unique challenges, but it is, nevertheless, an incredibly exciting, dynamic and fun world to be a part of, and it offers unlimited potential for personal and financial reward. Having made that first vital step of reading this book, now is the time to act. Don't doubt your abilities –you can do it!– and with the inside knowledge that you now have at your disposal, you can look forward to making your dream of becoming a truly successful event planner come true. So, get excited, get motivated and get out there! Oh, and have a great event!

Jorge Zurita

LEGAL DISCLAIMER AND TERMS OF USE AGREEMENT

The information contained in *How to Become a Successful Event Planner* represents a comprehensive collection of proven strategies which the book's author personally used to set up and run a successful event planning business. The advice, hints, tips and suggestions offered are merely recommendations by the author, who offers no guarantee that reading this book will bring about similar results to his own.

While all reasonable efforts have been made to ensure that the contents of this book and any accompanying materials are current, accurate and complete, neither the author nor the publisher accepts any claims or warranties in respect to the content itself, in relation to any unintentional errors or omissions which the book may contain, or which might arise either directly or indirectly as a result of any individual's use of the contents. In addition, they do not guarantee that the material contained within the book is suitable for any particular purpose or in any particular situation or circumstance. Should readers choose to apply any of the ideas contained within the material, they do so of their own volition and while accepting full responsibility for any outcome.

The material contained within *How to Become a Successful Event Planner* may refer to information, products, services or websites which are provided by third parties and over which the author and publisher have no control. The inclusion of such material is solely an expression of the author's own personal views and in no way constitutes its endorsement. The author and publisher of this guide, therefore, do not accept any responsibility or liability for the accuracy, completeness, performance, or effectiveness of such information, products, services, or websites, or in relation to the reader's subsequent use of them.

Before using any of the information or resources contained within this book, readers are advised to seek the advice of competent legal, accounting, or other appropriate professionals.

INDEX

21210776R00201

Made in the USA
Lexington, KY
03 March 2013